Praise for Brian Leaf's *Top 50 Skills* Series

Top 50 Skills for a Top Score: SAT Math

"What a surprise, what a relief! An SAT guide that actually meets you where you are, talks to you with wit and compassion, and clears away the panic of test-taking. And, the writing is first-rate too. Bravo Brian Leaf."

Rebecca Pepper Sinkler, **former Editor**, *The New York Times Book Review*

"I enjoyed the informal writing style, and the flash cards for math are brilliant! Students are used to stacks of vocabulary words in preparation for the verbal portion of the test, why not drills on flash cards for the math section?"

Denise Brown-Allen, Ed.D., **Upper School Director, The Pingry School**

"If everyone starts using Brian's secrets and strategies, The College Board and ETS are going to have to rewrite the SAT!!"

Max Shelton, **George Washington University, Class of 2012**

Top 50 Skills for a Top Score: SAT Critical Reading and Writing

"Brian Leaf has hacked off the head of America's high school boogie man—the dreaded SAT. He clearly lays out how the test works, accessible preparation strategies, and how to maximize one's score. Any college applicant can benefit from his thoughtful and well-researched advice."

Joie Jager-Hyman, **former Assistant Director of Admissions, Dartmouth College, author of** *Fat Envelope Frenzy: One Year, Five Promising Students and the Pursuit of the Ivy League Prize*

"A long time ago, in an era far, far away, I took the SAT—and I can remember the pressure and anxiety of it like it was yesterday. Lucky for you modern-day seniors, Brian Leaf has written the SAT guide to end all SAT guides. He thoroughly demystifies the test and lays out the 50 skills you need to max out your score. Better yet, Mr. Leaf writes with such humor, wit, and unpretentious expertise that you'll find yourself reading this book just for fun. I did. It almost—almost—even made me want to take the SAT again."

Sora Song, **Senior Editor**, *Time Magazine*

"What's more scary than facing SATs? Or more boring than prepping for them? For a student swinging wildly between angst and ennui, the solution is Brian Leaf's *Top 50 Skills for a Top Score: SAT Critical Reading and Writing*. Leaf, himself a genius at connecting with teenagers, meets students at their level, and spikes every drill with common sense and comedy. I especially loved the Superbad Vocabulary section—not your usual stuffy approach to language deficit disorder. Guaranteed to relax and engage the most reluctant (or panicked) student."

Rebecca Pepper Sinkler, **former Editor**, *The New York Times Book Review*

Top 50 Skills for a Top Score: ACT Math

"Anyone even thinking of taking the ACT needs this short but targeted guide to the math section. You simply can't afford not to spend the time reading his laser sharp drills that break down every type of problem on the ACT, show the math behind each type, and then provide drill sections based on that skill set. Even poor math students can learn to recognize all the types of math on the ACT and learn the ropes enough to get most of the easy and medium questions right every time. Mr. Leaf's guide is even entertaining as he gives the skill sets names like "Green Circle, Black Diamond" to make it feel like you are skiing rather than slogging through lessons. If you want a short but concise guide to the ACT with every trick and mathematical explanation necessary to get a perfect score, this is the book for you. You may even actually LEARN real math in the process as Mr. Leaf's love of the subject shines through so you don't just feel you are learning for a test."

Dr. Michele Hernandez, author of the bestselling books *A is for Admission, The Middle School Years,* **and** *Acing the College Application*

"Brian Leaf knows how to talk with students and in his book, *Top 50 Skills for a Top Score: ACT Math,* you can hear his voice loud and clear. Students who follow Brian's 'Mantras' and work through the practice questions will gain confidence in their work, as well as improve their ACT scores."

Barbara Anastos, former Director, Monmouth Academy

"Feels like you have an insider divulging secrets from behind the walls of the ACT! At times going so far as to circumvent the math skills themselves, Brian gives practical tips and tricks specifically designed to outwit the ACT's formula, and he does it all with a sense of humor and fun. Nice job!"

Danica McKellar, actress (*The Wonder Years, West Wing***) and mathematician and author of** *New York Times* **bestsellers** *Math Doesn't Suck* **and** *Kiss My Math*

Top 50 Skills for a Top Score: ACT English, Reading, and Science

"This book is a good read even if you *don't* have to take the ACT."

Edward Fiske, author of the bestselling college guide, the *Fiske Guide to Colleges*

"The **specific** skills needed for the ACT, confidence building, stress-management, how to avoid careless errors . . . this book has it covered!"

Laura Frey, Director of College Counseling, Vermont Academy
Former President, New England Association for College Admission Counseling

McGraw-Hill Education Top 50 Skills for a Top Score:
ACT English, Reading, and Science

Second Edition

Brian Leaf, M.A.

New York | Chicago | San Francisco | Athens | London | Madrid

Mexico City | Milan | New Delhi | Singapore | Sydney | Toronto

1 2 3 4 5 6 7 8 9 0   CUS/CUS   1 2 1 0 9 8 7 6

ISBN   978-1-2595-8627-9
MHID   1-2595-8627-8

e-ISBN   978-1-2595-8628-6
e-MHID   1-2595-8628-6

ACT is a registered trademark of ACT, which was not involved in the production of, and does not endorse, this product.

McGraw-Hill Education books are available at special quantity discounts to use as premiums and sales promotions or for use in corporate training programs. To contact a representative, please visit the Contact Us pages at www.mhprofessional.com.

Contents

How to Use This Book

It's simple. The questions that will appear on your ACT are predictable. In this book, I will teach you exactly what you need to know. I will introduce each topic and follow it with drills. After each set of drills, check your answers. Read and reread the solutions until they make sense. They are designed to simulate one-on-one tutoring, like I'm sitting right there with you. Reread the solutions until you could teach them to a friend. In fact, do that. My students call it "learning to channel their inner Brian Leaf." There is no better way to learn and master a concept than to teach it!

Any new concept or question type that you master will be worth points toward your ACT score. That's the plan; it is that simple.

This book is filled with ACT Mantras. They tell you what to do and when to do it. This is the stuff that girl who got perfect 36s does automatically. The Mantras teach you how to think like her.

"Sounds good, but the ACT is tricky," you say. It is, but we know their tricks. Imagine a football team that has great plays, but only a few of them. We would watch films and study those plays. No matter how tricky they were, we would learn them, expect them, and beat them. ACT prep works the same way. You will learn the strategies, expect the ACT's tricks, and raise your score. Now, go learn and rack up the points!

Guessing

The ACT is not graded like a test at school. If you got 55% of the questions right on your sophomore English final, that'd be a big fat F. On the ACT Reading section, 55% of the questions right is a 21, the average score for kids across the country. If you got 70% of the questions right, that'd be a C− in school, but a nice 25 on the ACT, the average score for admission to great schools like Goucher and University of Vermont. And 85% correct, which is a B in school, is a beautiful 30 on the ACT, and about the average for kids who got into Tufts, U.C. Berkeley, University of Michigan, and Emory.

Use the above info to determine how many questions you need to answer on the ACT. If you want half correct, or 70% correct, don't rush just to finish. In school you might need to finish tests in order to do well; here you do not. You only need to get to all the questions if you are shooting for 31+.

If a question seems hard, take another look for what you are missing. Ask yourself, Which Skill can I use? What is the easy way to do this question? After you complete this book, you will know!

Remember, on the ACT you lose **no** points for wrong answers. Even if you are running out of time at question #30 out of 40, you must budget a few minutes to fill in an answer for the last 10 questions. It'd be crazy not to. Statistically, if you randomly fill in the last 10 ovals, you'll get 2 to 3 correct. That's worth about 2 points (out of 36) on your score! So keep an eye on the clock, and when there are a few minutes left, choose an answer for each remaining question.

About Brian Leaf, M.A.

Six, maybe seven, people in the world know the ACT like Brian Leaf. Most are under surveillance in Iowa, and Brian alone is left to bring you this book.

Brian is the author of *McGraw-Hill's Top 50 Skills* SAT and ACT test-prep series. He is also the author of *Defining Twilight: Vocabulary Workbook for Unlocking the SAT, ACT, GED, and SSAT* (Wiley, 2009) and director of the New Leaf Learning Center in western Massachusetts. He teaches ACT, SAT, and PSAT prep to thousands of students from throughout the United States. (For information, visit his website www.BrianLeaf.com.) Brian also works with the Georgetown University Office of Undergraduate Admissions as an Alumni Interviewer, and is a certified yoga instructor and avid meditator. Read about Brian's yoga adventures in *Misadventures of a Garden State Yogi*.

Acknowledgments

Special thanks to all the students of New Leaf Learning Center for allowing me to find this book. Thanks to my agent Linda Roghaar and my editor at McGraw-Hill, Anya Kozorez. Thanks to Pam Weber-Leaf for great editing tips, Julie Leaf for psychological material, Zach Nelson for sage marketing advice, Ian Curtis and Matthew Thompson for assiduous proofreading, Manny and Susan Leaf for everything, and of course, thanks most of all to Gwen and Noah for time, love, support, and, in the case of Noah, hexagon finding and rumpus time.

Thanks to the following individuals who generously allowed me to butcher their work into English section passages: Kyle Tucker (Pretest), Hallie Haas (Skill 1 and Essay Skills), Matthew Thompson (Skills 2 and 3), Rose Benjamin (Skill 4), Tani Goderez (Skill 5), Ian Curtis (Skill 7, Essay Solutions), David Rice (Skill 9), Gwen Leaf (Skill 11), Abby Spector (Skill 13), Noah Dirks (Skill 14), Rachel Olshansky (Posttest I), Alex Milne (Posttest II), and Katie Smith (Posttest III).

Thanks also to the following individuals who generously allowed me to adapt their work into Reading section passages: Matthew Thompson (Skill 18), Alex Milne (Pretest, Skill 20), Michael Brooks (Skill 21, Posttest I), Kyle Rodd (Skill 22, #1 to 3), Gwen Leaf (Skill 22, #4; Skill 36; Posttest II), Colette Husemoller (Skill 23), David Rice (Pretest, Skills 24 and 27), Richard Wylde (Skill 28), Manpriya Kaur Samra (Skill 29), and Riley Kirkpatrick (Posttest III).

Pretest

This Pretest contains questions that correspond to our 50 Skills. Take the test, and then check your answers with the answer key on page 16. The 50 Skills that follow contain more detailed solutions as well as instructions and drills for each type of question on the ACT.

I. English Read the following passage.
Then, for each underlined part, consider the alternatives in the right-hand column and select the best answer.

It was a Monday morning in 2006, and I <u>am</u> Kyle
                                          1
Tucker the politician and intellectual, the defiant

liberal embarking on his first day of what would be

an illustrious political career. I, with several other

interns, <u>were arriving</u> at the "Bermuda Government
          2
Offices." We entered the lobby, dispensing

automatic "good mornings" and "hellos" (and the

occasional "what's up" reserved for the younger,

more friendly looking politicians). I approached the

bulletin board that held <u>your</u> summer destiny.
                          3
Jostling amongst other eager students, my eyes read

the dreadful words "Kyle Tucker—Assistant to the

Assistant to the Assistant Secretary of Security

Services."

"No, No, No!" I thought. <u>Nevertheless,</u> I got angry—
                          4
blood rushed to my head and my knees went weak.

My dreams of valiantly arguing the righteous cause

in Parliament were evaporating before my eyes. Not

<u>me, the budding politician, an</u> assistant to the
5
assistant to the assistant? Rage manifested within

me. I was no subordinate. Besides, I hated filing

and data entry. I was a politician!

① Ⓐ NO CHANGE
   Ⓑ was
   Ⓒ were
   Ⓓ have been

② Ⓕ NO CHANGE
   Ⓖ had been arrived
   Ⓗ was arriving
   Ⓙ were being arriving

③ Ⓐ NO CHANGE
   Ⓑ one's
   Ⓒ my
   Ⓓ whose

④ Ⓕ NO CHANGE
   Ⓖ But
   Ⓗ Still
   Ⓙ OMIT the underlined portion.

⑤ Ⓐ NO CHANGE
   Ⓑ me the budding politician an
   Ⓒ me the budding politician an,
   Ⓓ me the budding politician; an

I found my department, and I was immediately
                   6
given a list of mundane tasks. My thoughts went

between two poles: the government in serious need

of fixing, and the humiliation of filing. I was young,

but I understood every aspect in the government.
                                        7
My emotions went from anger to embarrassment to

sadness, then back to anger. At some point before

midday, I began thinking seriously about quitting.

"The Assistant's office, its right downstairs," I
                         8
thought. But I feared the words "I'll never quit." I

feared the gossip ". . . that Tucker kid quit his job . . .

looooser." I saw my mom's eyes and heard both of
                                9
my uncles' laughter. I was on page two of the Fire
    9
Station Monthly Expenditures data form when I

cracked.

What I said to my neighbor intern who worked next
                     10
to me, I don't recall. Something like, "Bathroom . . .
 10
I'll be quick . . . sorry." Climbing the metal stairs,

the intern supervisor's cubicle was two flights up.
            11
I remember staring at the man sitting there

expectantly, the curiously look on his face, and
                   12
then down at my hands, then at the Ministry exit

6. Which of the following alternatives to the underlined portion would NOT be acceptable?

  F. department: and I was

  G. department; I was

  H. department and was

  J. department. I was

7. A. NO CHANGE

  B. the government offered

  C. of the government

  D. for the government

8. F. NO CHANGE

  G. office; its

  H. office, it's

  J. office

9. A. NO CHANGE

  B. moms eyes and heard both of my uncles

  C. mom's eyes and heard both of my uncle's

  D. mom's eyes and heard both of my uncles

10. F. NO CHANGE

  G. neighbor intern next to me,

  H. neighbor intern

  J. neighbor, the intern next to me

11. A. NO CHANGE

  B. the cubicle of the intern supervisor

  C. I made a beeline to the intern supervisor's cubicle, which

  D. the intern supervisors cubicle, which

12. F. NO CHANGE

  G. quizzical

  H. stormy

  J. questionable

doors. I tried to will myself toward the glass doors.

"Now," I thought. But I couldn't.
      13
Freedom was just twenty quick steps away, but I

couldn't do it. I turned and walked back down the

hall.
14
15 And so I continued my work, and I learned a lot

that summer. It turned out I didn't know

everything, in fact I knew barely anything of

Bermuda's government. All I had known of local

politics to that point had been gleaned from my

parents' political banter, lopsided as it was.
                                      16

13 If the writer were to delete the underlined sentence, the paragraph would lose

- Ⓐ an important detail
- Ⓑ a transition from one sentence to the next
- Ⓒ some of its personal tone
- Ⓓ nothing at all, since this sentence is out of place

14 The writer wishes to add details that emphasize his trip back to his filing. Which would best accomplish this?

- Ⓕ hall, down the harsh metal stairs, straight to the Filing Room, then to my filing.
- Ⓖ hall, feeling the approval of my family.
- Ⓗ hall, knowing that one day I would do more than just file.
- Ⓙ hall, once again angry, yet perhaps more humble.

15 Suppose the writer had been assigned to write a brief essay about internship opportunities in Bermuda. Would this essay fulfill the assignment?

- Ⓐ Yes, because the essay describes his reaction to his assignment.
- Ⓑ Yes, because the essay indicates the effect of internships on young people in Bermuda.
- Ⓒ No, because the essay restricts its focus to the writer's internship experience.
- Ⓓ No, because the essay does not describe how the writer learned from his internship.

16 Ⓕ NO CHANGE
- Ⓖ lopsided
- Ⓗ lopsided as the banter was being
- Ⓙ lopsided as it's

II. **Reading** Read each passage and answer the questions that follow.

HUMANITIES: This passage is adapted from the article "Chuck Palahniuk Is Larger Than Life," by David Rice.

Starting with the ascent of the film adaptation of his novel *Fight Club* to the status of—the case could be made—*the* film of Generation-Y, following through the success of subsequent
5   novels *Choke*, *Lullaby*, and *Diary*, and then blossoming in last year's infamous bouts of fainting at public readings of a short story from his *Haunted* collection, Chuck Palahniuk has become a phenomenon as a personage and
10 performer, not only as a writer.

Palahniuk has become an American cult figure, thanks to his notably well maintained website (which actually calls itself "The Cult"), his father's recent murder at the hands of a crazed ex-convict,
15 and his outlandish research tactics, such as recent claims that, in preparation for *Rant*, he actually participated in a recreational car crashing club that features prominently in the novel. "Four times," he shrugged at another interview. "It was
20 fun. A great way to meet people. I loved demolition derby when I was a kid."

It is thusly apropos and perhaps a little snarky that Palahniuk now offers us his newest work, *Rant*, in the form of an "oral biography" of a
25 deceased character who has attained legendary stature.

Over the course of the novel—slick, suspenseful, and gruesome enough to devour in a single sitting—we come to know the title character. We
30 get to know him, like we get to know Palahniuk himself, better and better, or feel we do, but never actually meet him. His childhood friends and enemies (as they're demarcated) relate the mythos of his early days, his city friends tell
35 of his incarnation after leaving home, and his parents twine throughout, shedding whatever light they can on their son's unique dynamism and offering anecdotes to illustrate what, as far as they can tell, went wrong.

17   The main theme of this passage concerns the

(A) difficult life of a troubled author

(B) public persona of Chuck Palahniuk

(C) differences between Palahniuk's *Fight Club* and *Rant*

(D) challenges of presenting an "oral biography" of a deceased character

18   Which of the following best describes the author's feelings about the novel *Rant*?

(F) Confused awe

(G) Snarkiness

(H) Appreciation

(J) Respect mixed with concern

19   As it is used in line 34, the word "mythos" most nearly means

(A) legends

(B) ropes

(C) rebirths

(D) lies

20   According to the passage, the novel *Rant* tells the story of its main character through accounts from all of the following EXCEPT

(F) childhood teachers

(G) city friends

(H) childhood enemies

(J) his parents

21   In the context of the passage, the author implies that it is appropriate that *Rant* present the biography of a legendary character because

(A) the novel is gruesome

(B) the novel sheds light on the lead character's charismatic presence

(C) its author despises mythic tales

(D) Palahniuk is himself very prominent

SOCIAL SCIENCES: This passage is adapted from the article "An Analysis of Meadville's Struggling Main Street District," by Alex Milne.

A Main Street is the business and social center of an American small town. Meadville's "Main Street" district has seen better days. Most local sources agree the cause of Meadville's economic
5 hardships came from the loss of industries such as Talon Zipper and Avtech, and the loss of major railroad infrastructure.

The absence of industry was especially crippling since Meadville was (and to some extent, still is)
10 a manufacturing town. Further, it has been proposed that the loss of Meadville's status as a railroad hub caused damage to Meadville's appeal as a cultural district as well. The rails were no longer a viable form of transportation,
15 therefore slowing tourism. This lack of tourists hastened the decline of the downtown; traveling Americans rapidly had fewer and fewer reasons to pass through Meadville.

The problem with Meadville's downtown district
20 is, simply, not enough people shop there. Would-be patrons bypass Meadville for three main reasons. First, they don't have enough money to shop at the boutique stores found there—51% of Crawford County residents are middle/low
25 income, and 22% are at or below the national poverty line. Second, Meadville has few events and institutions thought of as "destinations" and is 45 minutes from any major metropolis. Third, the convenience, price, and selection at many of
30 the large box stores in Vernon Township direct traffic away from stores in the downtown district.

Meadville is one of the first small communities to receive funding from a national organization known as the Main Street Project. The Project
35 involved funding the hiring of a "Main Street Manager" to facilitate improvements to the downtown. In addition, downtown businesses have a few major assets to counterbalance their problems. Meadville is in a beautiful, rural
40 location. It has a charming, unique, and historic architecture. It's home to Allegheny College. And it's located conveniently close to I-79. It's also, both fortunately and unfortunately, a very inexpensive place to own a business.

22 In terms of mood, which of the following best describes the passage?

(F) Informative and sober

(G) Cautious but hopeful

(H) Distraught

(J) Apologetic and resolute

23 The main purpose of the passage can best be described as an effort to

(A) explain the appeal of American Main Streets

(B) explore the reasons for Meadville's struggling Main Street district

(C) examine contributing causes to the loss of Meadville's railroad infrastructure

(D) describe how Meadville's downtown has changed over the years

24 Which of the following statements best describes the structure of this passage?

(F) It contains a highly detailed anecdote that the author uses to prove a point.

(G) It presents logical analysis of the root causes of the economic hardships of Meadville's Main Street.

(H) It compares and contrasts the two major reasons for the economic difficulties of Meadville's Main Street.

(J) It begins with an impassioned plea for help and ends with encouraging news.

25 The phrase "loss of major railroad infrastructure," as it is used in lines 6 and 7, most specifically refers to

Ⓐ declines in profits of the railroad sector

Ⓑ sizable delays experienced by trains traveling through Meadville

Ⓒ decline of railroad use and facilities in Meadville

Ⓓ lack of shopping happening in Meadville

26 As it is used in line 16, the word "hastened" means

Ⓕ slowed

Ⓖ sped up

Ⓗ stalled

Ⓙ affordable

27 According to the last paragraph, which of the following statements would the author most likely make with regard to Meadville?

Ⓐ While Meadville's downtown had struggled, it has come a long way and is quickly recovering.

Ⓑ While Meadville's downtown has struggled, there are possibilities for recovery.

Ⓒ Meadville's downtown had struggled until it was revived by the Main Street Project.

Ⓓ Meadville's struggles have taught the business community valuable lessons that will lead to future economic growth.

28 Which of the following does the author cite as a reason why people do not shop in downtown Meadville?

Ⓕ It is far from another city.

Ⓖ It has no significant Main Street.

Ⓗ The county's residents have the money to shop at other, more expensive stores.

Ⓙ Meadville's rural location draws them away from downtown.

29 Which of the following best describes the author's tone in the final sentence of the passage?

Ⓐ Angry but regretful

Ⓑ Ironic

Ⓒ Sullen but resolved

Ⓓ Apologetic

III. Science Read the passage and answer the questions that follow.

Lake Alexander existed between 9400 and 12,800 years ago in southern Canada. The lake was formed when a large glacier flattened the land and created a dip below sea level. Soil excavated from the area where the lake stood reveals information about the time period that the sediments were deposited. Figure 1 shows a cross section of the sediments (sand and gravel and brown till) and bedrock in the area. Figure 2 shows the copper levels of groundwater taken from samples of the top 45 m of sediment at 2 sites along the same cross section. In general, copper enters groundwater through corrosion of household plumbing systems or erosion of natural copper deposits. Smaller copper levels indicate greater distance from urban areas and from natural copper deposits.

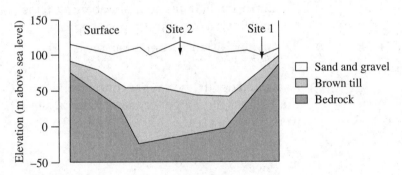

Figure 1

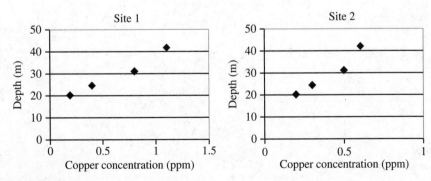

Figure 2

30 Based on the data in Figure 2, at sites 1 and 2 the deposit of lowest copper concentration in the groundwater was recorded at a depth of

- (F) 5 m
- (G) 20 m
- (H) 24 m
- (J) 50 m

31 According to Figure 1, which of the following has the thinnest deposit?

- (A) Sand and gravel at site 1
- (B) Sand and gravel at site 2
- (C) Brown till at site 2
- (D) Bedrock at site 1

32 According to Figure 1, as the thickness of the brown till deposit increases from site 1 to site 2, the thickness of the sand and gravel above it

- (F) increases
- (G) remains the same
- (H) decreases
- (J) first decreases, then increases

33 If a sample were taken at site 2 at a depth of 35 m, it would most likely show a copper concentration closest to

- (A) 1.0 ppm
- (B) 0.8 ppm
- (C) 0.55 ppm
- (D) 0.25 ppm

34 Based on the data in Figure 2, the largest natural copper deposit most likely existed

- (F) near the surface of site 1
- (G) near the surface of site 2
- (H) deep at site 1
- (J) deep at site 2

35 If the copper present in the samples has been there since before the area was Lake Alexander, what likely contributed to the presence of the copper?

- (A) Corrosion of household plumbing systems only
- (B) Erosion of natural copper deposits only
- (C) Corrosion of household plumbing systems and erosion of natural copper deposits
- (D) Greater distance from urban areas

36 At a given depth, the copper concentrations at site 2 versus the copper concentrations at site 1 were

- (F) the same
- (G) lower
- (H) higher
- (J) sometimes higher and other times lower

37 According to Figure 1, which of the following graphs best represents the *elevations*, in meters above sea level, of the top of the sand and gravel layer at sites 1 and 2?

Ⓐ

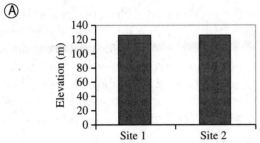

Ⓑ

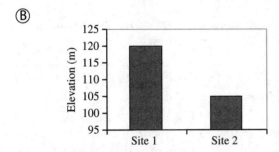

Ⓒ

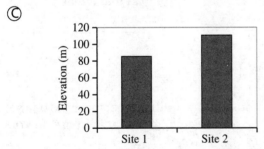

Ⓓ

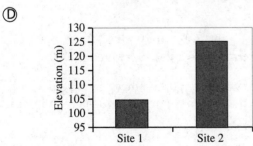

IV. Writing Test Read the directions below. Then read the prompt and use 40 minutes to write an essay.

Driver's License

In several states, legislatures have debated whether high school students should be required to demonstrate a passing grade average in school in order to take their driver's license examination. Obviously measuring responsibility would be helpful in the decision whether to award someone with a driver's license, but the question is, do high grades actually correlate to responsible driving? In your opinion, should high school students be required to demonstrate a passing grade average in order to take their driving test? Given the responsibly required to safely operate a motor vehicle, it is worth examining this issue.

Read and carefully consider these perspectives. Each suggests a particular way of thinking about the relationship between grades, responsibility, and receiving a driver's license.

Perspective One	Perspective Two	Perspective Three
Failing grades indicate irresponsibility and likely an irresponsible driver.	Grades and responsible driving are not related, so the requirement would be unfair.	Responsible driving requires skills like coordination and attention span that are not directly measured by grades.

Essay Task

Write a unified, coherent essay in which you evaluate multiple perspectives on the relationship between grades, responsibility, and receiving a driver's license. In your essay, be sure to:

- analyze and evaluate the perspectives given;
- state and develop your own perspective on the issue; and
- explain the relationship between your perspective and those given.

Your perspective may be in full agreement with any of the others, in partial agreement, or wholly different. Whatever the case, support your ideas with logical reasoning and detailed, persuasive examples.

Planning Your Essay

Your work on these prewriting pages will not be scored.

Use the space below and on the back cover to generate ideas and plan your essay. You may wish to consider the following as you think critically about the task:

Strengths and weaknesses of the three given perspectives

• What insights do they offer, and what do they fail to consider?
• Why might they be persuasive to others, or why might they fail to persuade?

Your own knowledge, experience, and values

• What is your perspective on this issue, and what are its strengths and weaknesses?
• How will you support your perspective in your essay?

If you need more space to plan, please continue on the back of this page.

Answer Key

1. B
2. H
3. C
4. J
5. A
6. F
7. C
8. H
9. A
10. H
11. C
12. G
13. C
14. F
15. C
16. F
17. B
18. H
19. A
20. F
21. D
22. F
23. B
24. G
25. C

26. G
27. B
28. F
29. B
30. G
31. A
32. F
33. C
34. H
35. B
36. J
37. D
38–49. See answers in corresponding Skill sections on pages 102–124.
50. J

English

The ACT begins with a 45-minute English section. The questions in the English section test your ability to recognize and correct 15 kinds of grammatical errors. In the next 15 Skills I will show you exactly what you need to know. I will show you how to recognize each type of error and how to correct it. Each Skill has an ACT Mantra. The Mantra tells you what to look for and what to do. Learn them and your score will go way up, guaranteed!

By the way, in the English section, there are five passages, each with 15 questions. Some kids don't read the passage; they skip it and go right to questions. But my students always gain points when they read the passage first. Even though you are not being tested on reading comprehension, sometimes you need the context.

Subject/verb agreement is the most common type of ACT writing question. The key to these questions is to trust your ear. You know the error when you hear it. If something sounds wrong, it probably is. If something is difficult to read, it's probably wrong. The purpose of good grammar is to make a passage easy to read and understand. So if it's not, if it trips up your tongue, or if you can't get its meaning, don't say, "Boy, that sounds kinda funny, but I must be wrong." Say, "I can't understand this, so **it** must be bad grammar." Trust yourself. Notice where your tongue gets tied up, where you have to pause and say, "What the . . .?" That's where the error is.

In the drills that follow we will train your ear. In a sentence, the subject and the verb must match. There is no fancy rule that I need to teach you; you already know this stuff, just from speaking and reading. What I need to teach you is to train and then trust your ear and, when in doubt, to identify the subject of the verb. In this Skill, we'll look at some straightforward questions. In the next Skill, we'll look at the one trick that the ACT tries.

Let's take a look at this on the Pretest.

It was a Monday morning in 2006, and I <u>am</u> Kyle Tucker the politician and intellectual, the defiant liberal embarking on his first day of what would be an illustrious political career.

1. **A.** NO CHANGE
    B. was
    C. were
    D. have been

Solution: Trust your ear. "It was a Monday morning in 2006, and I <u>am</u> Kyle Tucker" does not sound correct. "It was Monday" implies that the "I am" should be the past tense, "I was." You can hear that if you know to listen for it. That's our goal, to train you to listen for it.

Correct answer: B.

ACT Mantra #1
When a verb is underlined, trust your ear. When in doubt, identify its subject and make sure singular/plural and tense match the subject.

Subject/Verb Agreement Drills

There is something delightfully bizarre in the art of improvisational theater. Not only <u>being it</u> [1] completely unexpected and full of anxious excitement, but oftentimes, the material that emerges is utterly ridiculous.

For me, improv <u>was</u> [2] hard at first. And scary. I <u>been</u> [3] in organized productions since I was seven and had since then conquered stage fright. However, before my first improv performances, my heart would race as it did when I <u>were</u> [4] seven.

The nervousness that came from not knowing what I <u>would say</u> [5] resulted in me groping about wildly. This, I learned, will not earn you the laughter of the audience. What will work, however, <u>are</u> [6] disregarding any preconception you have about having to be funny all the time, and letting yourself actually <u>be listening and react</u> [7] to those around you.

1.
- (A) NO CHANGE
- (B) being
- (C) is it
- (D) it

2.
- (F) NO CHANGE
- (G) were
- (H) began to be
- (J) had being

3.
- (A) NO CHANGE
- (B) had been
- (C) will have been
- (D) was

4.
- (F) NO CHANGE
- (G) would have been
- (H) have been
- (J) was

5.
- (A) NO CHANGE
- (B) said
- (C) would have said
- (D) would have been saying

6.
- (F) NO CHANGE
- (G) being
- (H) is
- (J) has been

7.
- (A) NO CHANGE
- (B) listen and react
- (C) listens and reacts
- (D) listen and be reacting

The One Subject/Verb Agreement Trick

Usually the ACT does not try to be very tricky, but they do love this one subject/verb agreement trick. Every test uses it at least once. And since we expect it, it's not tricky for us.

Did you catch it on the Pretest?

I, with several other interns, <u>were arriving</u> at the "Bermuda Government Offices."

2. **F.** NO CHANGE
    G. had been arrived
    H. was arriving
    J. were being arriving

Solution: I love these, they are tricky, but we know they are coming! The trick is that "interns" might look like the subject of the underlined verb, but "I" is the subject. "Interns **were** arriving" sounds correct, but the subject of the verb is "I," so it should be "I **was** arriving."

Correct answer: H.

"How can I ever tell that?" you say. Ahh, my friend, easy. A prepositional phrase, such as "with several other interns," NEVER counts as the subject. Prepositional phrases always begin with a preposition ("on," "above," "below," "with," "by," "during," "until," ... just Google "prepositions" for a full list) and end with a noun, such as "interns." Here are a few more prepositional phrases: "of awards," "with six kids," or "on the table."

So when you are identifying the subject of an underlined verb, if there is a prepositional phrase, cross it out! Then subject/verb agreement is obvious, and a "tricky question" becomes "easy"!

Jimmy ~~with his friends~~ walks
The number ~~of awards~~ proves
Billy ~~along with six kids~~ goes

ACT Mantra #2
When a verb is underlined, identify the subject and cross out any prepositional phrases; a prepositional phrase NEVER counts as the subject of the verb.

The One Subject/Verb Agreement Trick Drills

Cross out any prepositional phrases between the subject and verb, and underline the subject of the **bold verb** in each of the following sentences.

❶ Margarita, with her sisters, currently **runs** a marketing firm.

❷ The way of all samurai **is** a strict path.

❸ The boys, with their dog Alfred, **walk** to school.

❹ The PTA, through generous donations, **is** building a new school building.

Now, let's see this trick on a few ACT questions.

Grandma's procedure for baking <u>cookies have</u> been
1
written in my mind with dough and colored sugar.

After the sticks of butter <u>have softened</u>, mix with one
2
cup of sugar. Next, crack two eggs over the edge of

the bowl and toss the shells into the compost bin.

Add one teaspoon of vanilla. Then, one-half cup of

brown and white sugars <u>is</u> added, and stir. Add two
3
cups of flour, one teaspoon of salt, and one

teaspoon of baking soda, and stir. Then place the

dough in the freezer for one hour to harden. When

the cookies, baking on the middle rack of the oven,

<u>becomes ready</u>, your nose will tell you.
4

❶ Ⓐ NO CHANGE
 Ⓑ cookies; have
 Ⓒ cookies has
 Ⓓ cookies being

❷ Ⓕ NO CHANGE
 Ⓖ has softened
 Ⓗ were soft
 Ⓙ has been softened

❸ Ⓐ NO CHANGE
 Ⓑ is being
 Ⓒ will have been
 Ⓓ are

❹ Ⓕ NO CHANGE
 Ⓖ become ready
 Ⓗ had become ready
 Ⓙ was

Pronoun Clarity and Agreement

When a pronoun (such as "he," "she," "it," "they," "them," "him," or "her") is underlined, we must be totally sure what noun it is referring to. If it is unclear, in any way, it is incorrect. You're smart, so you might be able to figure out which noun a pronoun refers to, but ask yourself, If Borat were translating this sentence, what would he think? If it's at all unclear, it's wrong. Also, once you know what the pronoun refers to, make sure that it matches—singular or plural.

Let's see this on the question from the Pretest.

I approached the bulletin board that held <u>your</u> summer destiny. Jostling amongst other eager students, my eyes

3. **A.** NO CHANGE
B. one's
C. my
D. whose

Solution: We cannot be sure who "<u>your</u>" refers to, so it's wrong. Also, on the ACT, only use "you" or "your" if it is used consistently throughout the essay, and never switch between "you" and "one."

Correct answer: C

As you learn the English Skills, use them to analyze each underlined word. If the underlined word is a verb, ask, What is its subject? If it's a pronoun, ask, What does it refer to and does it match?

ACT Mantra #3
When a pronoun is underlined, we must be totally sure what noun it is referring to. If it is unclear in any way, it is incorrect. The underlined pronoun must also match (singular or plural) the noun that it refers to.

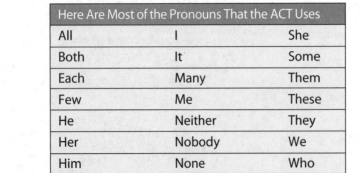

Here Are Most of the Pronouns That the ACT Uses		
All	I	She
Both	It	Some
Each	Many	Them
Few	Me	These
He	Neither	They
Her	Nobody	We
Him	None	Who
His	One	You

Pronoun Clarity and Agreement Drills

My grandma begins to flatten the dough with a wooden roller coated with flour. I devote my energies to the cookie cutters. <u>It is</u> all heaped
₁
together in an old plastic shopping bag. I become overwhelmed by my options and lay <u>them</u> all out.
₂
I love the simplicity of the star but am also intrigued by the complexity of the Santa. There's also the reindeer, the Christmas tree, and the sleigh. I select <u>those</u> cookie cutter that we will use and realize I
₃
have chosen mostly stars and Santas.

My next task it to decorate the newly born shapes with sugar. <u>She</u> takes a step back from the table
₄
and watches my eyes widen with excitement.
I begin to sprinkle red and green sugar arbitrarily across the top of <u>each</u> cookie. I release the crystals
₅
from my hand and wherever <u>it ends</u> up is fine with
₆
me. When I finally finish, my grandma tells me that they are "just perfect" and places them in the oven.

1.
- Ⓐ NO CHANGE
- Ⓑ It
- Ⓒ They being
- Ⓓ They are

2.
- Ⓕ NO CHANGE
- Ⓖ it
- Ⓗ each one
- Ⓙ those

3.
- Ⓐ NO CHANGE
- Ⓑ their
- Ⓒ each
- Ⓓ these

4.
- Ⓕ NO CHANGE
- Ⓖ My grandma
- Ⓗ He
- Ⓙ Who

5.
- Ⓐ NO CHANGE
- Ⓑ each and every
- Ⓒ this
- Ⓓ which

6.
- Ⓕ NO CHANGE
- Ⓖ those end
- Ⓗ they end
- Ⓙ those released crystals ends

Correct Transition Word

When a transition word (such as "although," "since," "but," "therefore," or "however") is underlined, see if it works in the flow of the sentence. Words like "therefore" express a direct cause and effect. Opposition words like "but" express a cause and effect where the second part opposes the first. For example:

Brian is funny; <u>therefore</u>, he makes you laugh.
   The second part results from the first part.
Brian is funny, <u>but</u> sometimes he is tired and dull.
   The second part opposes the first part.

When a transition word is underlined, check if it's the right transition word for the sentence. These are great. If you didn't know to look for them, you might miss 'em. You might think, "That was weird, but I guess it's okay." But it's not okay.

Let's take a look at the one from the Pretest.	**4. F.** NO CHANGE
	G. But
"No, No, No!" I thought. <u>Nevertheless</u>, I got angry—blood rushed to my head and my knees went weak.	**H.** Still
	J. OMIT the underlined portion.

Solution: "I got angry" follows the flow of the paragraph, rather than opposes it. But "nevertheless" implies opposition, so we want a different transition word, such as "therefore." All the choices are opposition words, so choice J (OMIT the underlined portion) is correct.

Correct answer: J

If we weren't looking for this, we might miss it, but we expect it and we catch it. This is where my job is easy; I just tell you what to look out for. Then you get them right, and it makes me look good!

ACT Mantra #4
**When a transition word (such as "although," "since," "but," "therefore,"
or "however") is underlined, see if it works in the flow of the paragraph.**

Direct Cause-and-Effect Words			Opposition Words		
Therefore	Thus	So	However	Although	But
Ergo	And	Since	Still	Though	
Because			Nevertheless	Even though	

Correct Transition Word Drills

Catherine the Great became empress of Russia in 1769. She guided Russia in a Golden Age for 34 years. <u>Otherwise,</u> this Golden Age was indeed a

1
time of prosperity for many, for others it was a time of oppression.

To many it appeared that Catherine was guiding Russia into prosperity, <u>though,</u> underneath the

2
surface, she disregarded the underprivileged. She took away their land and made it difficult for them to acquire an education. <u>Since</u> Catherine is known

3
as a just ruler, under her reign the peasantry actually suffered greatly.

<u>Whereas</u> Catherine effected many advancements

4
during her reign, such as founding the Russian Academy; however, these achievements targeted the nobility. <u>For example,</u> the schools she founded

5
were private with very expensive tuition. While Catherine did bring the Renaissance to Russia, peasants were too busy working to benefit from it. In truth, Catherine the Great took advantage of many to benefit the <u>few, therefore.</u>

6

❶ Ⓐ NO CHANGE
  Ⓑ Therefore
  Ⓒ Although
  Ⓓ And,

❷ Ⓕ NO CHANGE
  Ⓖ for
  Ⓗ therefore
  Ⓙ moreover

❸ Ⓐ NO CHANGE
  Ⓑ While
  Ⓒ Because
  Ⓓ Thus,

❹ Ⓕ NO CHANGE
  Ⓖ Since
  Ⓗ Considering
  Ⓙ DELETE the underlined portion.

❺ Ⓐ NO CHANGE
  Ⓑ Yet,
  Ⓒ Because of
  Ⓓ But,

❻ Ⓕ NO CHANGE
  Ⓖ few
  Ⓗ few of them
  Ⓙ few, yet

Relaxing Commas

Most kids see commas as a great mystery. But commas follow rules. They just indicate a pause; they are very relaxing. So when a comma is underlined on the ACT, ask yourself, Should there be a pause here? Use your ear—read it with and without a pause and see which works.

When you need to double-check your ear, here are the comma rules for the ACT:

1. Use a comma to set off a side note.
   Example: This book, as you know, is quite excellent.
   You can hear the pause before and after the side note "as you know."
   Example: You, Matt, are a great pianist.
   You can hear the pause before and after the side note "Matt."
   These sentences would sound bizarre if you read them without the pauses.

2. Don't use a comma if a phrase is essential to the sentence, because then it's not a side note.
   Example: The word "facile" comes from the Spanish word for easy.
   No commas because the word "facile" is essential, not a side note. If we took it out, the sentence would lose its meaning.
   Plus, if you try pausing before and after, it sounds weird.

There's one more rule that we need, which we'll do in Skill 6.

Let's take a look at the question from the Pretest.

Not <u>me, the budding politician, an</u> assistant to the assistant to the assistant?

5. **A.** NO CHANGE
   B. me the budding politician an
   C. me the budding politician an,
   D. me the budding politician; an

Solution: Try it with and without pauses. With pauses it sounds clear, and without pauses it sounds confusing and jumbled. "The budding politician" is a side note, inessential to the meaning of the sentence, so we need the commas.

Correct answer: A

ACT Mantra #5
When a comma is underlined on the ACT, ask yourself, Should there be a pause here? Read it with and without a pause and see which works. Commas (and pauses) are used to set off a side note.

Relaxing Commas Drills

My Room

My <u>room, is</u> always there for me. All my things are
<u>1</u>
there: the pictures, the books, the folders from
fourth grade. The walls are covered with <u>memories</u>
<u>2</u>
from my three-year-old birthday poster to faded
paintings done in seventh grade.

The rugs <u>underfoot being</u> always dusty, always
<u>3</u>
comforting, are a multicolor patchwork <u>of irregular</u>
<u>4</u>
<u>shapes.</u> Out the window is a familiar landscape,
<u>4</u>
always there, like an old friend that won't let me
down. The colors of the <u>wall blue</u> and red, are deep
<u>5</u>
rich colors that warm me and keep me safe.
Sometimes, <u>though</u> like on hot days, the deep
<u>6</u>
colors keep me cool.

The most special place in the whole <u>room, my bed.</u>
<u>7</u>
It's a place to relax and just be, a reassuring face in
a sometimes unfriendly world. The cozy blankets
are always ready to warm me; the pillow is a fluffy
cloud. My room is a special world all of my own.

1 Ⓐ NO CHANGE
   Ⓑ room,
   Ⓒ room is,
   Ⓓ room is

2 Ⓕ NO CHANGE
   Ⓖ memories;
   Ⓗ memories,
   Ⓙ memories, and

3 Ⓐ NO CHANGE
   Ⓑ underfoot, really
   Ⓒ underfoot are
   Ⓓ underfoot,

4 Ⓕ NO CHANGE
   Ⓖ of, irregular, shapes
   Ⓗ of, irregular shapes
   Ⓙ of irregular, shapes

5 Ⓐ NO CHANGE
   Ⓑ wall is blue
   Ⓒ wall, blue
   Ⓓ wall, being blue

6 Ⓕ NO CHANGE
   Ⓖ therefore,
   Ⓗ though;
   Ⓙ though,

7 Ⓐ NO CHANGE
   Ⓑ room is my bed
   Ⓒ room, being my bed
   Ⓓ room; my bed

Are You Independent?

I told you in Skill 5 that there was one more comma rule for the ACT. Here it is. When a phrase in a sentence does not complete a thought and leaves you waiting for the rest, you separate it from the rest of the sentence with a comma (or a dash or parentheses). When the phrase is a complete thought that could stand on its own, and does not leave you hanging, you separate it with a semicolon or a comma with "and."

The fancy term for a phrase that cannot stand alone is "dependent," and the fancy term for one that can is "independent." That makes sense, like when you have a job and learn to cook and can stand on your own, you are independent.

Commas, Dashes, Parentheses

He thought, as soon as he woke up, that he'd like to go back to sleep.
He thought—as soon as he woke up—that he'd like to go back to sleep.
He thought (as soon as he woke up) that he'd like to go back to sleep.

In all these examples, the phrase "as soon as he woke up" is dependent—it would not be a complete sentence alone. Therefore it is separated by commas, dashes, or parentheses. Technically, each of these has a subtly different use, but the ACT uses them interchangeably and **never** tests the differences between commas, dashes, and parentheses.

Semicolon

He woke up; he decided to go back to bed.
He woke up, and he decided to go back to bed.
He woke up. He decided to go back to bed.

Both parts of each of these sentences are independent and could stand alone, so they are separated by a semicolon, comma with "and," or a period.

Let's take a look at the question from the Pretest.

I found my <u>department, and I was</u> immediately given a list of mundane tasks.

6. Which of the following alternatives to the underlined portion would NOT be acceptable?
   F. department: and I was
   G. department; I was
   H. department and was
   J. department. I was

Solution: "I found my department" and "I was immediately . . . " are both complete thoughts that could stand alone; they are independent. Therefore, they must be separated by a semicolon, comma with "and," or a period. Using the process of elimination, choice F is the answer. I did not teach you about colons yet, so here goes: colons are used to separate a list or a clause that explains. Choice F would work if the second part of the sentence expounded on the first and did not have the "and," for example, "I found my department: it was the filing room."

Correct answer: F

ACT Mantra #6
**Phrases that can stand alone are separated with a semicolon,
comma with "and," or a period.**

Are You Independent? Drills

Jean Piaget popularized a theory of intellectual development; he taught that all children moved
<u>development; he taught that</u>
        ₁ all children moved
through a set pattern of development in a fixed
order. He called the four stages of <u>development; the</u>
        ₂
sensorimotor, the preoperational, the concrete
operational, and the formal operational.

Piaget's stages are often contrasted with those of
Erik Erikson. Erikson focused on how children
come to understand <u>themselves. And,</u>
        ₃
the world around them. His theory has eight <u>stages,</u>
                                ₄
<u>beginning</u> at birth and ending in late adulthood.
   ₄
The first four stages of Erikson's theory cover the
same ages as Piaget's four <u>stages; however, other</u>
                           ₅
than age of experience, the stages do not have an
obvious relationship to each other.

1 Which of the following alternatives to the underlined portion would NOT be acceptable?

  Ⓐ development. He taught that
  Ⓑ development—that
  Ⓒ development; teaching that
  Ⓓ development, teaching that

2 Ⓕ NO CHANGE
  Ⓖ development the
  Ⓗ development, the
  Ⓙ development; as the

3 Ⓐ NO CHANGE
  Ⓑ themselves; and
  Ⓒ themselves,
  Ⓓ themselves and

4 Ⓕ NO CHANGE
  Ⓖ stages; and begins
  Ⓗ stages, it begins
  Ⓙ stages; beginning

5 Ⓐ NO CHANGE
  Ⓑ stages, however, other
  Ⓒ stages, however. Other
  Ⓓ stages, however; other

Correct Preposition

The ACT calls this topic "correct idiom." I love their term; you just don't hear people using the word "idiom" nearly enough. It makes me think of *Monty Python and the Holy Grail* when Sir Lancelot receives a call of distress from the singing Prince of Swamp Castle. Lancelot's squire wants to come along for the daring rescue, but Lancelot says that he must rush the castle "in his own particular . . . idiom."

Instead of "correct idiom," which I can't say without laughing, I call it "correct preposition." I do this for two reasons:

❶ I'm not sure if I'd have to pay the ACT to use their term.
❷ The words that we are looking for are always prepositions, so it's much easier than looking for the "correct idiom."

Remember from Skill 2 that prepositions are words like "up," "above," "of," "into," "on," "below," "with," "by," "during," "until." You can Google "prepositions" for a full list. When a preposition is underlined, ask yourself if it's the correct preposition. How do you know? The correct one will make sense and sound smooth. The wrong one will sound weird or jarring. This is another great place to practice trusting your ear. If it sounds jarring, it's probably wrong. We'll train on the drills.

Here are some examples:

Correct:	Incorrect
Zann went **to** the movies.	Zann went **onto** the movies.
Giancarlo sat **on** the couch.	Giancarlo sat **in** the couch.
Malaria is a threat **to** travelers.	Malaria is a threat **of** travelers.
Focusing **on** your studies will bring you success.	Focusing **with** your studies will bring you success.

Let's practice on the question from the Pretest.

I was young, but I understood every aspect <u>in the government</u>.

7. **A.** NO CHANGE
   B. the government offered
   C. of the government
   D. for the government

Solution: "But I understood every aspect in the government" sounds weird. The aspects are not literally **in** the government; they are aspects **of** the government. "Every aspect of the government" sounds great. Trust your ear. This is a great Skill; knowing to watch for the correct preposition turns a hard question into easy points!

Correct answer: C

ACT Mantra #7
When a preposition is underlined, ask yourself if it is the right preposition to use.

Correct Preposition Drills

Feeling out of place at school and needing

something new, last January I started helping

<u>out on</u> Miss Kelly's study halls. Every Tuesday and
  1

Thursday, I'd read novels to eighth graders. If I

continued <u>in reading</u> the same page over and over
     2

again, enough times, they'd understand it.

One day the science teacher told me, beaming, that

one of my students had received a B <u>on</u> his
                  3

ecosystems and biomes test.

That student, Nick, never said a word <u>on</u> it to me,
                              4

even though he and I had spent a long time

studying the material together. Truthfully, I don't

know if he even cared <u>for</u> the grade, but I had never
                  5

been prouder.

Tutoring those kids turned out <u>on being</u> one of the
                  6

most rewarding experiences I had ever had. I still

felt a little out of place at school, but I had a

purpose, and I was excited when I woke up every

day, especially on Tuesdays and Thursdays.

❶
- Ⓐ NO CHANGE
- Ⓑ out to
- Ⓒ out in
- Ⓓ out into

❷
- Ⓕ NO CHANGE
- Ⓖ to read
- Ⓗ on reading
- Ⓙ the reading of

❸
- Ⓐ NO CHANGE
- Ⓑ with
- Ⓒ about
- Ⓓ in

❹
- Ⓕ NO CHANGE
- Ⓖ by
- Ⓗ for
- Ⓙ about

❺
- Ⓐ NO CHANGE
- Ⓑ about
- Ⓒ what
- Ⓓ on

❻
- Ⓕ NO CHANGE
- Ⓖ in being
- Ⓗ for
- Ⓙ to be

It's Me

The ACT tests two special pronouns. If there were a million of these special rules, we might be in trouble; but there are two. Memorize the rules for these two special pronouns and you gain points!

The ACT likes "me." They also love "I." They love to ask you if "I" or "me" is correct in a sentence. That's great, because we have an incredibly easy and effective way to determine which is correct. If "I" is underlined, test it by putting it first or dropping the other person and then trusting your ear. You can also use this trick for "who" versus "whom," "he" versus "him," etc.

The second special pronoun that the ACT loves to test is "its" versus "it's." Usually, apostrophe s ('s) means possession, as in "Brian's book." But "it's" is a special case and means the contraction for "it is," while "its" is possessive, like "its color is red."

"It's" means "It is."
"Its" is possessive, like "that tree is nice, and I like **its** colorful leaves."

That's it. Drill and memorize these, and you'll gain points.

Let's try this on the question from the Pretest.	**8. F.** NO CHANGE **G.** office; its **H.** office, it's **J.** office
At some point before midday, I began thinking seriously about quitting. "The Assistant's <u>office, its</u> right downstairs," I thought.	

Solution: First, this is a great review of Skill 6. "The assistant's office" is not complete; it cannot stand alone. So it must have a comma instead of a semicolon. Second, "its" is possessive, but we want the contraction for "it is," so choice H is correct.

Correct answer: H

ACT Mantra #8
If "I" or "me" is underlined, test it by putting the I/me first or drop
the other person and trust your ear. If "its" or "it's" is underlined,
remember that "it's" means "it is," and "its" is possessive, like "that
tree is nice; I like <u>its</u> colorful leaves."

Our "Put the I/me first or drop the other person and trust your ear" strategy also applies to

I vs. Me
He vs. Him
She vs. Her
We vs. Us
They vs. Them
Who vs. Whom

It's Me Drills

Sometime in college, <u>Manuel and me</u> had heard
                          1
that an enlightened person is so relaxed that their
eyes are always half closed. I doubt <u>its true</u>, but at
                                        2
the time we believed it.

A few years later we were traveling and met a guru,
a very advanced yoga teacher. "The key to a yoga
practice," he said, "is to follow <u>its</u> call." We all sat
                                     3
together awhile and talked.

The scene was perfect. Someone brought tea to
<u>Manuel and I</u>. The guru wore all white and sandals
     4
and spoke in wise aphorisms.

I was listening to a story about <u>he and his student</u>,
                                       5
when I realized that the guru's eyes were half
closed. "Wow," I thought, "he is enlightened."

Later, about to leave, I said, "I'd love to attend one
of your yoga classes." "That would be wonderful,"
he responded, "except, I'm not teaching this month.
I just had eye surgery, and <u>who</u> can see with these
                                 6
darn drops in their eyes!"

1
- (A) NO CHANGE
- (B) Manuel and I,
- (C) Manuel and I
- (D) me and Manuel

2
- (F) NO CHANGE
- (G) if there is truthfulness to this
- (H) it's true
- (J) its the truth

3
- (A) NO CHANGE
- (B) it's
- (C) their
- (D) they're

4
- (F) NO CHANGE
- (G) Manuel and myself
- (H) Manuel and, I
- (J) Manuel and me

5
- (A) NO CHANGE
- (B) his student and himself
- (C) him and his student
- (D) his student and he

6
- (F) NO CHANGE
- (G) whom
- (H) which person
- (J) whose

A Few More Rules

Each of the eight Skills that you've learned so far appears on every single ACT. The four topics in this Skill appear less often, but often enough that you should memorize them.

❶ **Apostrophe s**
Examples: the teacher's book—one teacher has a book
the teachers' book—more than one teacher possesses the book
Remember from Skill 8 that "its" is possessive and "it's" means "it is."
Also "who's" means "who is," and "whose" is possessive.

❷ **ly**
Sometimes, the ACT adds an "ly" when we don't need it. It's tough to spot if you're not watching for it, easy if you are! "Nasty, tricksy" ACT makers, but we know and expect their tricks, so we get the questions right!

❸ **"Which" is for things; "who" is for people.**
Examples: Sierra is a girl **who** runs every day.
Computers, **which** can be very helpful, have become easier to use.

❹ **Certain words go together, such as**
Neither . . . nor
Either . . . or
Not only . . . but also

Example: I like **neither** ham **nor** venison.

Now, let's look at the example from the Pretest.

I saw my <u>mom's eyes and heard both of my uncles'</u> laughter.

9. **A.** NO CHANGE
   B. moms eyes and heard both of my uncles
   C. mom's eyes and heard both of my uncle's
   D. mom's eyes and heard both of my uncles

Solution: Since there are two uncles, "uncles' laughter" is correct. "Mom's" is also correct. So there is no error.

Correct answer: A

ACT Mantra #9
"My uncle's books" means one uncle has books, and "my uncles' books" means that two or more uncles have the books. Watch for an unneeded "ly." "Who" is for people, and "which" is for things. Watch for pairs of words such as "not only . . . but also" and "either . . . or."

A Few More Rules Drills

The *Boredoms* is a noise band <u>which</u> I've actually
                                    1
listened to. I can't say that I constantly walk
around with them in my earphones, but I'm
somewhat <u>familiarly</u> with their sound and have
          2
identified certain moments when they are just the
thing.

What I admire about their project is that they can
not only deconstruct <u>and</u> also reconstruct a song at
                       3
will. Sometimes the sound devolves into arrhythmic
mutterings, and other times the disparate pieces
find one another and form something <u>their own</u>,
                                       4
and a throbbing, perplexing song emerges.

While their sound is every bit as difficult as most
grind <u>groups sounds</u>, they are special for not taking
        5
themselves so seriously. If you're going to do crazy
stuff like this, I'd say you should do it for fun.

1
- Ⓐ NO CHANGE
- Ⓑ who
- Ⓒ whom
- Ⓓ whose

2
- Ⓕ NO CHANGE
- Ⓖ familiarity
- Ⓗ familiar
- Ⓙ recognizable

3
- Ⓐ NO CHANGE
- Ⓑ but
- Ⓒ yet
- Ⓓ while

4
- Ⓕ NO CHANGE
- Ⓖ it's own;
- Ⓗ his own:
- Ⓙ whose own,

5
- Ⓐ NO CHANGE
- Ⓑ group's sounds
- Ⓒ groups' sounds
- Ⓓ groups sound's

Direct, to the Point, Not Redundant

"Named must your fear be before banish it you can."
Jedi Master Yoda

Great advice. True for Jedi training. True for the ACT. But unless you're an 800-year-old Jedi Master, don't try speaking or writing in the passive voice; the ACT always favors the active voice. "Active voice" is just fancy grammar language for "be direct and to the point."

The ACT is not testing to see if you are the next Jedi, nor is it testing to see if you are the next William Shakespeare. They are merely testing to see if you can write a clear and concise memo from your cubicle at Dandar Mifflin Corporation. So the secret rule for English ACT questions is to choose the answer that is most clear, concise, direct, and nonredundant.

Let's see this on the Pretest.

What I said to my <u>neighbor intern who worked next to me,</u>

10. **F.** NO CHANGE
    G. neighbor intern next to me,
    H. neighbor intern
    J. neighbor, the intern next to me

Solution: The word "neighbor" implies the person "who worked next to me," so the other words are redundant and unneeded. Ax them. The ACT likes crisp and clear. We always want the answer that is most clear, concise, direct, nonredundant, and of course grammatically correct.

Correct answer: H

ACT Mantra #10
The ACT likes crisp and clear; we always want the answer that is most clear, concise, direct, and nonredundant.

Direct, to the Point, Not Redundant Drills

Begin to take deep relaxed <u>breaths, breathing in a</u> <u>relaxed way.</u> Mentally scanning your body,
$$\overline{1}$$

consciously relax your muscles, one at a time, from your toes to the top of your head. <u>Stress and</u> <u>tension are breathed out</u> with each exhalation.
$$\overline{2}$$

With each inhalation, breathe in relaxation.

After your muscles have become <u>relaxed, and less</u> <u>tight</u>, allow your mind to relax. Notice anxieties and
$$\overline{3}$$

mental tensions. Visualize the incoming breath dissolving buried mental tensions. Then, <u>imagining</u> <u>that your mind is like a clear blue sky, it is that you</u>
$$\overline{4}$$

see the thoughts as slowly floating clouds.

Relax here awhile. Then, when you are <u>ready and</u> <u>all set</u>, gently stretch your body in the way that
$$\overline{5}$$

feels most natural for you. Notice how you feel and make the intention to return to this feeling whenever you need some stress relief. Then, open your eyes and <u>with open-eyes</u> slowly sit up.
$$\overline{6}$$

1
- Ⓐ NO CHANGE
- Ⓑ breaths, and breathing in a relaxed way.
- Ⓒ breaths, in a relaxed way.
- Ⓓ breaths.

2
- Ⓕ NO CHANGE
- Ⓖ Let stress and tension be the things breathed out
- Ⓗ Breathe out stress and tension
- Ⓙ In the breathing, let it be stress and tension that are breathed out

3
- Ⓐ NO CHANGE
- Ⓑ relaxed
- Ⓒ relaxed, with less tension
- Ⓓ relaxed, and are less tight

4
- Ⓕ NO CHANGE
- Ⓖ it being that you are imagining that your mind is like a clear blue sky,
- Ⓗ imagining that your mind is like a clear blue sky, you
- Ⓙ imagine that your mind is like a clear blue sky and

5
- Ⓐ NO CHANGE
- Ⓑ set and ready
- Ⓒ all ready and set
- Ⓓ ready

6
- Ⓕ NO CHANGE
- Ⓖ with opened-eyes
- Ⓗ with eyes being open
- Ⓙ OMIT the underlined portion

Misplaced Phrases

Look at this sentence:

A beloved children's story, Ethel read *The Three Little Pigs* to her son.

The sentence makes it sound like Ethel is a beloved children's story. That's how Borat would read it. "A beloved children's story" is misplaced. It should be closer to the thing it's describing, "*The Three Little Pigs*." On the ACT, a descriptive phrase should always be very close to the thing that it describes. The ACT uses this type of question **several times** per test.

Let's see this on the Pretest.

Climbing the metal stairs, <u>the intern supervisor's cubicle</u> was two flights up.

11. A. NO CHANGE
   B. the cubicle of the intern supervisor
   C. I made a beeline to the intern supervisor's cubicle, which
   D. the intern supervisors cubicle, which

Solution: The way the sentence is set up, it seems that "Climbing the metal stairs" is describing the intern supervisor's cubicle. Of course it is not; you're smart and know that, but someone translating the sentence would be misled. That's the point of good grammar, to make writing completely clear. So "Climbing the metal stairs" should be as close to the thing that it describes ("I") as possible, and choice C is the best. Choice C also makes the sentence more clear and direct.

This question is a great place to use the process of elimination. If ever you are confused by a question, identify an error that needs fixing and eliminate choices that don't fix the error. Choices A, B, and D all have a misplaced phrase. Even if you can't identify choice C as the right answer, you can get it by the process of elimination!

Correct answer: C

ACT Mantra #11
A descriptive phrase on the ACT must be clearly associated with (and usually placed right next to) the noun described.

Misplaced Phrases Drills

My grandparents' <u>farm was the opposite of my</u>
    ₁
<u>apartment in the city, with the fresh air of its</u>
    ₁
<u>open pasture.</u> I remember eating early morning
    ₁
cornflakes with brown sugar and advising on
Grandpa's game of solitaire. This was followed
by midmorning breakfast <u>with Grandma of Rice</u>
    ₂
<u>Krispies and toast with plenty of jam.</u>
    ₂
Grandma and I would go to the neighborhood
ladies' brunch, but first, we'd bring lunch pails
<u>in the fields baling hay out to the workers.</u> Those
    ₃
summers I learned to knit. I remember Grandma's
limitless repertoire of knitting, embroidery, crochet,
and sewing projects.

<u>I savored the familiar smell of</u> Grandpa's work
    ₄
shirt. I remember his enormous hands and the lines
that told the stories of decades of satisfying hard
work. <u>With rhythm and simplicity, the memory of</u>
    ₅
<u>the time</u> I spent with Grandma and Grandpa gives
    ₅
me a sense of security, nurturing, and calm.

1 Ⓐ NO CHANGE
   Ⓑ farm was like the opposite to my city apartment, and the fresh air of the open pasture
   Ⓒ farm, was the opposite of my apartment in the city with the fresh air of the open pasture
   Ⓓ farm, with the fresh air of its open pasture, was the opposite of my apartment in the city

2 Ⓕ NO CHANGE
   Ⓖ of Rice Krispies and toast with plenty of jam of Grandma's.
   Ⓗ with Grandma; we ate Rice Krispies and toast with plenty of jam
   Ⓙ and Grandma's eating Rice Krispies and toast with plenty of jam

3 Ⓐ NO CHANGE
   Ⓑ in the fields' hay baling out to the workers
   Ⓒ out to the workers baling hay in the fields
   Ⓓ out in the fields baling hay to the workers

4 Ⓕ NO CHANGE
   Ⓖ With its familiar smell, I savored
   Ⓗ With its smell, I familiarly savored
   Ⓙ The familiar smell, I was always savoring

5 Ⓐ NO CHANGE
   Ⓑ The memory of the rhythm and simplicity of the time
   Ⓒ With rhythm and simplicity, the time of the memory
   Ⓓ With rhythm and simplicity, I remember the time

Word Choice

In ninth grade my best friend got hold of a thesaurus. Trying to impress our English teacher, he replaced a bunch of the words in his essay with fancier words. The problem was that the fancier words didn't always quite fit, and the essay sounded crazy.

The ACT loves to do that too. They just click on the thesaurus button and substitute a word that means nearly the same but does not fit in the sentence. This is definitely another "trust your ear" topic. If it sounds crazy, it is. Don't say, "That sounds kinda funny, but I must be wrong." Say, "That sounds weird, so let's see if the choices give something that sounds better."

Let's take a look at the question from the Pretest.

I remember staring at the man sitting there expectantly, the <u>curiously</u> look on his face, and then down at my hands, then at the Ministry exit doors.

12. F. NO CHANGE
     G. quizzical
     H. stormy
     J. questionable

Solution: Your ear can definitely tell that "the <u>curiously</u> look" sounds weird and is wrong. This is actually a nice review of Skill 9, "Sometimes the ACT adds an "ly" that does not belong." Tough to catch for someone who wasn't expecting it, but easy for us! So now that we know it sounds weird, let's see how the answers sound. Only choice G makes sense in the context of the paragraph. The man does not have a stormy (violently angry) or questionable (disputed) look on his face; he has a quizzical (inquiring) look.

Correct answer: G

ACT Mantra #12
Make sure that the underlined word fits into the context of the sentence.

Word Choice Drills

The hit TV show *Entourage* <u>demonstrates</u> a young
₁
movie star navigating life in Hollywood. In the
show, the main character, Vince, faces <u>contests</u>
₂
from other actors to get the best roles. Yet, he
remains grounded and calm.

In one episode, when he was <u>known to</u> go on a late-
₃
night talk show, his advisors told him to prep
interesting topics to discuss. But he just decided to
go on the show and be present. It's this very
attitude that makes him so successful with so <u>much</u>
₄
loyal fans. He is present to opportunity as it arises.

Vince is not <u>inefficient</u>, he just listens to his gut
₅
rather than being sucked into the games of
Hollywood. In another episode, he turned down a
movie deal that he did not really want in hopes of a
<u>long-shot</u> deal. He did this because waiting for the
₆
long-shot felt energizing and right and gave him a
huge <u>trickle</u> of excitement, whereas taking the sure-
₇
thing movie felt wrong.

1. Ⓐ NO CHANGE
   Ⓑ teaches
   Ⓒ portrays
   Ⓓ proves

2. Ⓕ NO CHANGE
   Ⓖ competition
   Ⓗ trials
   Ⓙ disputing

3. Ⓐ NO CHANGE
   Ⓑ agreed to
   Ⓒ scheduled to
   Ⓓ apparently to

4. Ⓕ NO CHANGE
   Ⓖ much a number of
   Ⓗ many
   Ⓙ fully many

5. Ⓐ NO CHANGE
   Ⓑ indifferent
   Ⓒ absent
   Ⓓ caring

6. Ⓕ NO CHANGE
   Ⓖ lengthy-shot
   Ⓗ full of unsureness
   Ⓙ elongated shot

7. Ⓐ NO CHANGE
   Ⓑ tweak
   Ⓒ reaction
   Ⓓ surge

Flow

Flow questions test you on the flow of an essay. They ask about the logical progression and organization of ideas in the essay, including questions about the introductory paragraph, body paragraphs, transition sentences, concluding paragraph, order of sentences, and order of paragraphs. These are the same Skills that we'll review later when we discuss writing the essay. We'll go into tons of depth for each of these topics in that section. For now, let's see how the questions in this section show up.

Here's the question from the Pretest.

I tried to will myself toward the glass doors. "Now," I thought. But I couldn't. Freedom was just twenty quick steps away, but I couldn't do it.

13. If the writer were to delete the underlined sentence, the paragraph would lose
   A. an important detail
   B. a transition from one sentence to the next
   C. some of its personal tone
   D. nothing at all, since this sentence is out of place

Solution: Read the sentences before and after the underlined portion. Then use the process of elimination on the choices:

A. ~~an important detail~~—Nope, it's not an important detail.
B. ~~a transition from one sentence to the next~~—No, it does not transition from one thing to another.
C. some of its personal tone—Yes, he tells the reader his thoughts, very personal.
D. ~~nothing at all, since this sentence is out of place~~—Nope, the underlined sentence is not out of place. It fits into the flow of the paragraph very well.

Correct answer: C

> **ACT Mantra #13**
> **For "flow" questions, use the process of elimination.**

Flow Drills

Every July, my family spends a few weeks on a "clothing-optional" beach on Martha's Vineyard.
1
This section of Lucy Vincent Beach is the final stop on a half-mile stretch of sand, and it's the place my family has been planting their multicolored beach umbrellas since the 1970s. [2]

As a little kid, I played happily, unconcerned about the nudity. My attitude toward the nude beach changed when I was twelve. Nothing around me made me feel that going to a nude beach was anything other than weird, and I abandoned my family's beach community. I kept away for three
3
years, but the summer when I was fifteen, on the third day of our vacation (I still do not remember how it happened), it just felt right to get up and start walking down to the far end of the beach. Everyone loves the beach. Fifty yards before my
4
family's rainbow-colored beach umbrella, I ran to my "clothing-optional" family.

1 Which choice would best tie the introduction of this essay to the essay's concluding sentence?
- Ⓐ NO CHANGE
- Ⓑ special beach
- Ⓒ the Lucy Vincent Beach
- Ⓓ multicolored umbrella

2 At this point, the writer is considering adding the following true statement:
> The 1970s saw an oil crisis and the growth of the environmental movement.

Should the writer make the addition here?
- Ⓕ Yes, because the sentence provides more information about the 1970s.
- Ⓖ Yes, because the sentence provides important background information about the author.
- Ⓗ No, because the sentence is not supported by evidence to back it up.
- Ⓙ No, because the sentence distracts from the paragraph's focus.

3
- Ⓐ NO CHANGE
- Ⓑ (Begin new paragraph) In keeping away
- Ⓒ (Begin new paragraph) I kept away
- Ⓓ (Do NOT begin new paragraph) In keeping away

4
- Ⓕ NO CHANGE
- Ⓖ Most people love the beach.
- Ⓗ Everyone's love is the beach.
- Ⓙ DELETE the underlined portion.

Goal Questions

Several questions per test ask you to decide which answer choice would best accomplish a certain goal. I have seen this type of question boggle students. Usually, all the choices sound pretty good. **The key to this type of question is to choose the one choice that achieves the very specific goal stated in the question.** All the answers might sound pretty good, but only one will meet the **goal**. Let's take a look at this on the Pretest. Once you know to look for the one choice that meets the specific goal stated in the question, these are easy!

Let's take a look at the goal question on the Pretest.

I turned and walked back down the <u>hall</u>.

14. The writer wishes to add details that emphasize his trip back to his filing. Which would best accomplish this?
   F. hall, down the harsh metal stairs, straight to the Filing Room, then to my filing.
   G. hall, feeling the approval of my family.
   H. hall, knowing that one day I would do more than just file.
   J. hall, once again angry, yet perhaps more humble.

Solution: The specific goal for the question is to "add details that emphasize the writer's trip back to his filing." Choice F adds details about his walk back, and choices G, H, and J do not. They are interesting and refer to details in the essay but do not meet the **goal** specifically stated in the question. I love this strategy; once you know to look for the goal, these questions are easy!

Correct answer: F

ACT Mantra #14
For "goal" questions, choose the one answer choice that achieves the very specific GOAL stated in the question.

Goal Questions Drills

Frederick Douglass was born on February 14, 1818. 1 This "Sage of Anacostia" is one of the most influential figures in African-American history. He was an ardent activist and reformer of human rights.

Douglass was born into slavery. In 1838, at the age of 20, he successfully escaped his Maryland plantation and settled in Massachusetts. There he told his story and became a respected anti slavery lecturer.

Douglass' most famous written work is his autobiography *Narrative of the Life of Frederick Douglass, an American Slave*. 2 The book's vivid account informed the public and fueled the anti slavery movement.

Douglass went on to publish several newspapers, including the *North Star* whose motto was "Right is of no Sex—Truth is of no Color—God is the Father of us all, and we are all brethren." 3

1. At this point the writer wants to add a sentence that links the first two sentences. Assuming all are true, which of the following would best accomplish this?

(A) Doing some of his most influential work from his home in Anacostia, Washington DC.

(B) Born a slave, he wound up a revered reformer.

(C) Because he lived for the last 20 years of his life in Anacostia, Washington DC, he is associated and often nicknamed for that place.

(D) The exact date of his birth is not known.

2. In this paragraph, the writer intends to briefly describe the content of the autobiography. Which one of the following best accomplishes the writer's intention?

(F) He went on to revise and republish the autobiography two times.

(G) The book details Douglass' life from birth to escape from slavery.

(H) The book received positive reviews and became an immediate bestseller.

(J) Critics doubted its authenticity, skeptical of such eloquent language from someone who had not received a formal education.

3. Which of the following true statements, if inserted here, would best conclude the essay as well as maintain the tone established in the introduction?

(A) Douglass also published *The New National Era*.

(B) These publications affected many readers and helped advance the anti slavery movement.

(C) This "Sage of Anacostia" overcame great obstacles to become one of the most important reformers of United States history.

(D) And, truly, Douglass lived this motto.

Yes or No?

Several questions per test ask you to decide if a passage accomplished a certain intention. This is a great opportunity for the process of elimination. Decide if it did or did not, and then decide which reason is most correct. Every ACT has several of these questions, and many kids consider them the hardest type. But when you are used to the language, they are easy!

Did you catch it on the Pretest?

15. Suppose the writer had been assigned to write a brief essay about internship opportunities in Bermuda. Would this essay fulfill the assignment?
  A. Yes, because the essay describes his reaction to his assignment.
  B. Yes, because the essay indicates the effect of internships on young people in Bermuda.
  C. No, because the essay restricts its focus to the writer's internship experience.
  D. No, because the essay does not describe how the writer learned from his internship.

Solution: Would the essay fulfill an assignment about internship opportunities in Bermuda? It did mention an internship in Bermuda, but only one. It was not about various opportunities, just about Kyle's one internship. It was a great essay, but it was not about internship opportunities.

Once you know the answer is no, decide which reason is better. Choice C is perfect; it did not meet the assignment because it restricts its focus to the writer's internship. Choice D is incorrect because he did describe what he learned from his internship, but that does not matter to the assignment. Make sure that the answer you choose meets the whole assignment (all the words), and not just the first few.

Correct answer: C

ACT Mantra #15
**For a yes/no question, choose an answer that applies to the entire question
and not just a few words of it.**

Yes or No Drills

[1] Many actors devote themselves entirely to studying Shakespeare, and there are schools explicitly for this purpose. These schools work to produce Shakespearean actors. But, ironically, we do not know what training an actor actually received in Shakespeare's time.

The truth is that there is very little known about the techniques used to train Shakespearean actors. We do not know the curriculum used. Nor do we know the duration of training. [2]

We do know that Shakespeare's plays include sword fights, brawls, dances, and music. We therefore conclude that actors needed to be familiar with and were trained in swordplay, stage combat, dancing, and music.

The theater even incorporated realistic bloodshed. For example, sheep's or pig's organs were used in murder scenes, and sheep's blood was splashed about on swords and wounds. [3]

❶ Suppose the writer had decided to write an essay that summarizes the curriculum at the top three schools for studying Shakespearean acting. Would this essay fulfill the writer's goal?

Ⓐ Yes, because the essay describes the training required of Shakespearean actors.

Ⓑ Yes, because the essay includes the techniques and courses that these schools teach.

Ⓒ No, because the essay argues that we know almost nothing about the training of Shakespearean actors.

Ⓓ No, because the essay limits its focus to a general overview and does not go over the training at the top three schools.

❷ The writer is considering deleting the phrase "The truth is that" from the first sentence of this paragraph. If the writer were to delete this phrase, would the meaning of the sentence change?

Ⓕ Yes, because the reader might doubt the validity of the assertion.

Ⓖ Yes, because the sentence would become much weaker.

Ⓗ No, because the phrase is an example of wordiness and is unneeded in the sentence.

Ⓙ No, because the following paragraph disproves the statement anyway.

❸ Suppose the author had intended for the final paragraph to serve as a conclusion for the essay. Would the paragraph fulfill this goal?

Ⓐ Yes, because the reader learns new information about stage combat.

Ⓑ Yes, because the paragraph is full of powerful details.

Ⓒ No, because the paragraph does not wrap up the essay as a whole.

Ⓓ No, because the paragraph lacks sufficient details to back up its claim.

How to Think Like a Grammar Genius

You've now learned all the Skills that you need for the ACT English section. The Mantras remind you what to do and when to do it. Learning Mantras is like learning martial arts. Practice until they become part of you, until you follow them naturally: when you see an underlined verb, you look for its subject; when you see an underlined transition word or preposition, you ask yourself if it fits; when you see an underlined pronoun, you check for clarity and agreement; you watch for an unneeded "ly"; you train and trust your ear; and you use the process of elimination. This will raise your ACT English score dramatically, and it will improve your actual writing too.

Let's make sure you've memorized and integrated the Mantras. Check the box next to each Skill when you have mastered it. Reread any Skill sections that you need to.

☐ **Skill 1.** When a verb is underlined, trust your ear. When in doubt, identify its subject and make sure singular/plural and tense match the subject.

☐ **Skill 2.** When a verb is underlined, identify the subject and cross out any prepositional phrases; a prepositional phrase NEVER counts as the subject of the verb.

☐ **Skill 3.** When a pronoun is underlined, we must be totally sure what noun it is referring to. If it is unclear in any way, it is incorrect. The underlined pronoun must also match (singular or plural) the noun that it refers to.

☐ **Skill 4.** If a transition word (such as "although," "since," "but," "therefore," or "however") is underlined, see if it works in the flow of the sentence.

☐ **Skill 5.** When a comma is underlined, ask yourself, Should there be a pause here? Read it with and without a pause and see which works. Commas (and pauses) are used to set off a side note.

☐ **Skill 6.** Phrases that can stand alone are separated with a semicolon, a comma with "and," or a period.

☐ **Skill 7.** When a preposition is underlined, ask if it is the right preposition to use.

☐ **Skill 8.** When "I" or "me" is underlined, try putting the I/me first or drop the other person, and trust your ear. "It's" means "It is," and "its" is possessive, like "that tree is nice; I like its colorful leaves."

☐ **Skill 9.** "My uncle's books" means one uncle has books, and "my uncles' books" means that two or more uncles have books. Watch for an unneeded "ly." "Who" is for people, and "which" is for things. Watch for pairs of words such as "not only . . . but also" and "either . . . or."

☐ **Skill 10.** The ACT likes crisp and clear; we always want the answer that is most clear, concise, direct, and nonredundant.

☐ **Skill 11.** A descriptive phrase on the ACT must be clearly associated with (and usually placed right next to) the noun described.

☐ **Skill 12.** Make sure that the underlined word fits in the context of the sentence.

☐ **Skill 13.** For "flow" questions, use the process of elimination.

□ **Skill 14.** For "goal" questions, choose the one answer choice that achieves the very specific GOAL stated in the question.

□ **Skill 15.** For a yes/no question, choose an answer that applies to the entire question and not just a few words of it.

Let's apply these on the question from the Pretest.

All I had known of local politics to that point had been gleaned from my parents' political banter, <u>lopsided as it was</u>.

16. **F.** NO CHANGE
    G. lopsided
    H. lopsided as the banter was being
    J. lopsided as it's

Solution: The underlined phrase sounds pretty good. Let's try the choices in case there is an even better option. Choice G makes no sense in the sentence. Choice H is too wordy and "was being" sounds terrible. Choice J is incorrect since "it's" means "it is," which sounds wrong and does not match the past tense of the rest of the sentence. So choice F is correct.

Let's apply the Mantras to see why: the pronoun "it" clearly refers to "banter," the comma correctly represents a pause, "was" matches the tense of the rest of the sentence, and the underlined clause is right next to "banter," which it describes. You don't need to do all that though. You can just use the process of elimination and say, "The underlined words sound good, and the answer choices sound awful, so NO CHANGE."

Correct answer: F

How to Think Like a Grammar Genius Drills

In a famous well-known scene in the movie *Jerry*
___
1

Maguire, one character tells another that he loves

her and that she completes him. These concepts of

love, completing someone, and even marriage have

meant different things at different times of history.
___
2

Only recently have people married for love alone.

Originally, people married for survival—they live in
___
3

tribes and depend on each other for safety, food,
___
3
and shelter.

In the last 100 years, as the industrial revolution

has made life for some easier the idea of marriage
___
4
for love has come about. Its now frowned upon in
___
5
some cultures to marry for financial and social gain.

People hope to marry the person who completes
___
6
them, cares for them, likes them, and stands by
___
7
them; the person that makes them feel at ease.
___
7
Before people married for need, and now they

marry for need of love.

---

❶
- Ⓐ NO CHANGE
- Ⓑ famous, well known scene,
- Ⓒ famous scene
- Ⓓ famous and well known scene

❷
- Ⓕ NO CHANGE
- Ⓖ to history
- Ⓗ in history
- Ⓙ historically speaking

❸
- Ⓐ NO CHANGE
- Ⓑ were living and depending in tribes
- Ⓒ live in tribes and are depending
- Ⓓ lived in tribes and depended

❹
- Ⓕ NO CHANGE
- Ⓖ easier,
- Ⓗ easier;
- Ⓙ easier, and

❺
- Ⓐ NO CHANGE
- Ⓑ It's
- Ⓒ It was
- Ⓓ Presently, it is

❻
- Ⓕ NO CHANGE
- Ⓖ whom
- Ⓗ whose
- Ⓙ which

❼
- Ⓐ NO CHANGE
- Ⓑ stands by them. The person
- Ⓒ stands by them—the person
- Ⓓ stands by them the person

Reading

In the next 12 Skills I will show you the four types of reading passages and seven types of questions that the ACT uses in the Reading section.

Many students believe that reading comprehension questions are tricky, with several answers that work. But in the next 12 Skills, I'll show you that they're not tricky and that, in fact, they're totally predictable. In English class you might discuss for 30 minutes what Walt Whitman meant when he wrote something, but on the ACT there can be only one right answer, no tricks, no debate. The reading passage will always provide clear proof for the correct answer. Your goal is to be a detective or a lawyer and find the proof. After learning these 12 Skills, you'll find the Reading section easy and predictable. Read, learn, and drill these Skills, and you'll raise your score, guaranteed!

Bold Introductions

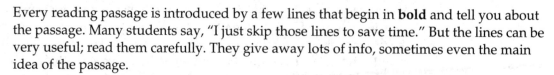

Every reading passage is introduced by a few lines that begin in **bold** and tell you about the passage. Many students say, "I just skip those lines to save time." But the lines can be very useful; read them carefully. They give away lots of info, sometimes even the main idea of the passage.

First, the lines tell you which of the four types of ACT passages you are about to read. Knowing the type gives you a bit of a hint:

- **Prose fiction**, which just means fiction, or stories, will definitely be followed by questions about characters' feelings and relationships.
- **Social science** and **humanities** passages are essays about things like history or art and will be followed by questions about details in the passage and about the writer's beliefs.
- **Natural science** passages will be about sciency stuff but will NOT expect you to know any science; everything will be explained in the passage, and questions will ask about details in the passage.

After telling you the type of passage, the intro lines give the title of the passage and occasionally a brief summary or note about a character. This gives away a ton of info and even helps you anticipate and therefore better understand the passage, which will help you stay focused while you read. (This is also a great strategy when reading your high school history text or your future college philosophy books; the intro sentences or italics can tell you a lot.)

Let's try this out on the bold intro from the Pretest.

HUMANITIES: This passage is adapted from the article "Chuck Palahniuk Is Larger Than Life," by David Rice.

17. The main theme of this passage concerns the
   A. difficult life of a troubled author
   B. public persona of Chuck Palahniuk
   C. differences between Palahniuk's *Fight Club* and *Rant*
   D. challenges of presenting an "oral biography" of a deceased character

Solution: The bold intro in this case pretty much gives us the answer to the first question. It tells us that the passage is adapted from the article "Chuck Palahniuk Is Larger Than Life." The last sentence of the first paragraph confirms that the passage is about the "larger than life" public persona of Chuck Palahniuk. We can eliminate the other choices because the passage is not about his difficult life, it does not compare *Fight Club* and *Rant*, and it does not mention challenges of presenting an "oral history." Each of these choices has words that appear in the passage, but only choice B is the main theme.

Correct answer: B

ACT Mantra #17
Always begin a reading passage by reading the bold intro.

Bold Introductions Drills

Each of the following is a bold intro to an ACT reading passage. What can you conclude from each?

① PROSE FICTION: This passage is adapted from the novel *Winson's Tuna Casserole* by D. A. Booch. The story is set in the mid-1990s in Hoboken, New Jersey, where the narrator and her friend have moved after graduating college.

④ NATURAL SCIENCE: This passage is adapted from *Life on Other Planets* by Isaac Schmumpkins. The narrator is Galileo Galilee, an astronomer, philosopher, and mathematician.

② SOCIAL SCIENCE: This passage is adapted from Josh Kutchai's biography *American Hero: The Story of Martin Luther King Jr.*

⑤ SOCIAL SCIENCE: This passage is adapted from Ron Hanake's *Darkest Night: America's Comic Book Obsession.*

③ HUMANITIES: This passage is adapted from the essay "Will Farrell: America's Jester or Clowning Genius?" by Ian Curtis, which appeared in *The Noynek University Review.*

⑥ HUMANITIES: This passage, which describes a young man's search for his sister, is adapted from the essay "The Post-War Years: Rebuilding and Reconnecting" by Justin Farmer-Van Wort.

The ACT Reading Meditation

After you have digested the bold intro, read the passage in a relaxed, yet very focused way. This is like meditating. When you notice your mind wandering, come back to the moment; bring your mind back to the reading. Anytime your mind wanders, bring it back. That will save time and energy and bring you closer to being a Zen master. For years, Zen monks in the mountains of Japan have been training with ACT reading passages.

Don't read to memorize details. Read to figure out the main idea and tone—what the passage is about and how the author feels about it. **When you notice the theme of a paragraph, circle a few key words that capture that theme.** Then when a question asks for details about that theme, you'll know where to look.

Also, and this is huge, I give you permission not to reread hard lines or lines that you spaced out for. This is especially important for perfectionists. Either we won't need the lines and the time rereading would have been wasted, or we will need them and we'll reread later, knowing the question and knowing what to look for. You never need any one particular sentence to get the main idea and tone. Main idea and tone are expressed throughout the passage.

One more thing. Many students worry, "Can I read this whole passage? It'll take 10 minutes." I felt the same way. Then one day I was like, "Wait, this is ridiculous, how long can it take?" So I timed myself. It took like 3 minutes! Try it, and you'll see. Even for a slow reader, the passage takes only a few minutes, especially if you use my "Don't Reread" strategy.

Let's take a look at the next question from the Pretest.

18. Which of the following best describes the author's feelings about the novel *Rant*?
   F. Confused awe
   G. Snarkiness
   H. Appreciation
   J. Respect mixed with concern

Solution: Use the key words that you've circled or scan the passage to find where the author mentions *Rant*. In the beginning of the last paragraph, the author describes *Rant* as "slick, suspenseful, and gruesome enough to devour in a single sitting." He read it in one sitting. Think of a book you devoured in one sitting; the author **appreciates** *Rant*. He does not mention being confused by it, he is not snarky (snide), and he does not express concern.

Correct answer: H

ACT Mantra #18

Read the passage looking for main idea and tone. That helps you stay focused; keep asking yourself, What are the main idea and tone? When you notice the theme of a paragraph, circle a few words that capture it. Don't try to memorize details, and don't reread hard lines. If you need them, you'll reread later when you know the question and what to look for.

The ACT Reading Meditation Drills

Read the following passage for main idea and tone, and when you notice the theme of a paragraph, circle a few words that capture it.

PROSE FICTION: This passage is adapted from "The Goodbye Kiss" by Matthew Thompson.

The *President Hoover* shoots a cloud of steam into the sky and sounds its horn as a final call. I lean against the railing on the upper deck, staring off into the cool San Francisco Bay. She waves to me, tears in her eyes, her light blue bonnet blowing in the wind, as she says her final goodbye to her new husband. I blow a kiss, filled with guilt, and the propellers begin to turn. The ship heads under the bridge, leaving behind the world I used to know.

Seven days of high seas, waves crashing against the hull and soaking the teak floors of the ship. A skyline emerges through the fog. Chinese junks and beggar sampans float past my porthole. Beggars and women selling chickens flood the streets of Shanghai, the modern skyscrapers soaring high above them. Han men and women dressed in their colorful costumes walk the cobblestone streets. As I pass restaurants and street vendors, an aroma of Hoisin sauce pervades the crisp air. I find myself mystified by such a strange new world, walking the streets aimlessly to capture its essence.

I am suddenly awakened from my dreams by a blast below me. The floor trembles and my two bedside lamps shatter over the carpet. Screams of terror fill Nanking Street. The rustic beauty that I saw the day before has vanished and out the window lie thousands, the streets stained red. Nowhere to run, I love you Margaret.

My heart continues to pound, but I am safe. Our ship sets sail as the flames encompass the city in the backdrop. Through the porthole, the world turns from horrifying red and orange to luscious green. Terraced rice fields cut through the thick tropical forest. I become immersed in a culture so vastly different than that of the Midwest, with only the crosses and steeples to bring me home. Meat cooked over an open fire. Dancing the Tinikling. Shell necklaces, leather bags, and hand-woven hats.

Women dress with only thick beaded necklaces and intricate henna tattoos covering their chests. The men, dressed in tribal gansas, return home from war and dance around an enemy's decapitated head. A canoe commemorates such a "special event," Igorots making beats with the brass rings dangling around their calves and feasting on spit-roasted pork. They accept me as their own, asking me to join in their festivities and abandon my Western dress. I laugh. I feel free.

Those eyes keep glaring. I stare back, accepting them as a normalcy, but soon memories of home creep back into my mind. Margaret. I picture her sitting in the orange corduroy armchair, playing Chinese checkers. How she must miss me, young and alone. Crying on Christmas, imagining me in a place beyond her isolated realm.

What's it generally about?

What's the tone/attitude/feeling?

"Facetious" Most Nearly Means

You've read the passage, continually asking yourself, "Self, what are the main idea and tone?" You've circled key words in each paragraph. Now, go to the questions. If the questions begin with the main idea, and you feel pretty sure what it is, answer it. If you feel unsure, do the "line number" and detail questions first. To answer "line number" questions, the ones that tell you what line number to look back at, go back and reread the lines. And for detail questions that do not give a line number, refer to your circled key words to find the location of the answer. By the time you've done all the detail and line number questions, you'll have reprocessed the passage and be even more sure of the main idea and tone. This is an awesome strategy that will definitely raise your score.

When you answer a detail or line number question, always go back and reread not only the lines that the question refers to but also at least three lines before and after. The answer usually comes before or after. If I say, "Vince Vaughn, the big man, is one facetious dude," I am probably expounding on what I said in the previous line, or on what I'm about to say in the next line. The next line would probably be: "Don't you agree, he's just the funniest guy," and now we know that "facetious" means "funny." That's how the ACT works. They always explain tough words nearby!

In this Skill, we'll practice the first type of line number question. These questions quote a word or phrase and ask you what the author "most nearly means."

Let's take a look at the question from the Pretest.

19. As it is used in line 34, the word "mythos" most nearly means
   A. legends
   B. ropes
   C. rebirths
   D. lies

Solution: This is a type of line number question, a question that asks what a word or phrase means. To answer it, go back to the line and reread a few lines before and a few lines after. These lines indicate that friends, enemies, and family are relating the details of the character's life. Earlier, the passage also indicated that the character was legendary. So choice A is the best answer.

You can also answer this question by crossing out the word in the passage, deciding, in context, what word you'd like to replace it with, and then looking at the choices to see which one fits best.

Correct answer: A

ACT Mantra #19
**To answer a "most nearly means" question, reread a few lines
before and a few lines after.**

"Facetious" Most Nearly Means Drills

HUMANITIES: This passage is adapted from the essay "The Three Battles of Beowulf" by Ciara Bede.

The events described in the epic poem "Beowulf" take place after the Anglo-Saxons had begun to put down roots in England, in the late 500s through the 600s AD. They had moved from
5 Scandinavia and northern Germany.

Scholars agree that "Beowulf" can be divided into the three main battles of the poem. The first battle was with Grendel. As Beowulf and his men passed the hours of darkness in the
10 "safety" of Herot, the palace of King Hroðgar, Grendel entered the hall and attacked. Asleep, the men were defenseless, and Grendel devoured one of Beowulf's soldiers. Awakened by the noise, Beowulf feigned sleep and leaped
15 up, unexpected, grabbing Grendel's arm in a strong hold. The two had an epic battle, tearing the great hall apart, until ultimately Beowulf ripped Grendel's arm from his body and Grendel fled home to die.

20 The second battle was with Grendel's mother, who sought revenge. After celebrating Grendel's death, Hroðgar and his men fell asleep, and Grendel's mother appeared. She brutally attacked the hall and killed Hroðgar's most
25 trusted warrior. Again a battle ensued, and again Beowulf was victorious, beheading her. King Hroðgar was, characteristically, never stingy with accolades. He rewarded Beowulf with the sword Naegling, a family heirloom.

30 Beowulf returned home from Herot and became king. Many years later, a slave stole a golden cup from a dragon. The dragon sought revenge and the third, and final, battle ensued. With the help of a young warrior, named Wiglaf, Beowulf
35 defeated the dragon, but eventually died from wounds from the battle.

❶ As it is used in line 3, the phrase "put down roots" most nearly refers to

(A) establishing agriculture

(B) harvesting crops

(C) settling an area

(D) clan warfare

❷ By "passed the hours of darkness" (line 9), the author most nearly means that they

(F) arrived at morning

(G) traveled beyond the dark forest

(H) emerged into safety

(J) spent the night

❸ As it is used in line 14, the word "feigned" means

(A) stopped

(B) faked

(C) fainted

(D) did not expect

❹ As it is used in line 16, the term "epic" most nearly means

(F) a battle between sworn enemies

(G) massive and destructive

(H) time-honored

(J) very close

❺ As it is used in lines 27 and 28, the phrase "never stingy with accolades" most nearly means that King Hroðgar

(A) was free with gifts of appreciation

(B) slew Beowulf with his family sword

(C) named Beowulf his successor

(D) gave freely to charity

Direct Info

"He's playing **fetch** . . . with my kids . . . he's treating my kids like they're dogs."

Debbie, *Knocked Up* (Universal Pictures, 2007)

This type of question asks you to directly retrieve info from the passage. No interpretation, no inferring. The key here is to be a dog; just play fetch. And be a lawyer; if you are given a line number, read a little before and a little after the line number and find evidence for an answer. If you are not, look at your circled key words and find where the question is answered in the essay. Either way, prove your answer with info from the passage.

You'll notice that the answer to a question will almost always come right before or right after the line number or detail referred to. And the correct choice will usually rephrase the correct answer. Usually, it won't be word for word from the passage. For example, instead of saying "studying will improve your ACT score," the correct answer choice might say "test results are raised by repeated practice." The two phrases mean the same thing but use different words.

Let's see this on the question from the Pretest.

20. According to the passage, the novel *Rant* tells the story of its main character through accounts from all of the following EXCEPT
   F. childhood teachers
   G. city friends
   H. childhood enemies
   J. his parents

Solution: Always look for the evidence in the passage. Be a lawyer; find proof. This is true for all types of questions, and especially for these direct info questions. Search your circled key words or scan the passage for info about *Rant*'s main character. The last paragraph states, "His **childhood friends and enemies** (as they're demarcated) relate the mythos of his early days, his **city friends** tell of his incarnation after leaving home, and his **parents** twine throughout, shedding whatever light they can." So we learn about him through city friends, childhood enemies, and his parents. We do not hear from childhood teachers. Don't be fooled by the word "childhood," which does appear in the paragraph but not with "teachers." Make sure all of an answer works and not just the first few words.

Correct answer: F

ACT Mantra #20
For a direct info question, always read before and after a line number or key word and find proof. The correct answer will usually rephrase the way the answer is stated in the passage.

Direct Info Drills

NATURAL SCIENCE: This passage is adapted from the essay "A Comparison of the Loma Prieta and Kocaeli Earthquakes," by Alex Milne.

The 1999 Kocaeli earthquake and the 1989 Loma Prieta earthquake both occurred along similar transform plate boundaries, causing similar strike and slip seismic disturbances. The Loma Prieta earthquake occurred along the San Andreas fault between the Pacific and North American plates, and the Kocaeli along the North Anatolian fault between the Eurasian plate and Anatolian block. The quakes were similar in magnitude, with the Kocaeli incident being the larger.

Although the epicenter of the Loma Prieta earthquake was close to both Santa Cruz and San Francisco (and that is where much of the damage occurred) it was significantly outside dense population centers. The Kocaeli earthquake occurred both around and in urban centers (the epicenter was *in* the city of Izmit), causing greater damage. From a human perspective, the severity of an earthquake relates to how many people are there to experience it.

The greatest danger of an earthquake comes from the failure of the structures people surround themselves with. So, the most important precaution a society can take in preventing losses from catastrophic earthquakes is to ensure structures are appropriately prepared to endure seismic activity according to the geologic material they rest on, or, even better, to ensure nothing is built on significant faults in the first place. A secondary measure is to ensure appropriate systems and organizations are in place to respond to earthquakes.

1. The author draws which of the following comparisons between the Kocaeli and the Loma Prieta earthquakes?

   (A) The Kocaeli and the Loma Prieta had very different magnitudes.

   (B) The Kocaeli and the Loma Prieta earthquakes both occurred in California.

   (C) The magnitude of the Kocaeli earthquake was larger than that of the Loma Prieta.

   (D) The Kocaeli and the Loma Prieta earthquakes caused very different slip seismic disturbances.

2. According to the passage, the most important precaution that a society can take to prevent loss from an earthquake is to

   (F) avoid building on major fault lines

   (G) keep populations of cities low

   (H) strengthen structures built on fault lines

   (J) carefully evaluate building materials

3. According to the passage, the epicenter of the Loma Prieta earthquake was

   (A) in the middle of Santa Cruz

   (B) considerably outside an urban center

   (C) near Kocaeli's epicenter

   (D) in the city of Izmit

4. The passage indicates that the North Anatolian fault must be closest to

   (F) Santa Cruz

   (G) the San Andreas fault

   (H) San Francisco

   (J) Izmit

5. In the context of the third paragraph, when the author states "geologic material they rest on," he is referring to

   (A) the incline of the land

   (B) the materials used in a building's foundation

   (C) stress a building can endure

   (D) the possible presence of a fault line

What Are You Trying to "Suggest"?

This type of question asks you what the author "suggests" or "implies," or what we can "infer." Skill 20 concerned questions that ask for information directly from the passage, like "Where was the epicenter of the earthquake?" But "suggest" questions ask for information that was not necessarily directly stated but was directly hinted at.

When students see these, they think that they have to pull some crazy AP English logic. But, actually, the key is to **not** overthink the answer. For a "suggest" question, we must still have proof from the passage. The correct answer for any ACT question, even this type, should always rephrase what was directly stated or hinted at in the passage.

Here's the question from the Pretest.

21. In the context of the passage, the author implies that it is appropriate that *Rant* present the biography of a legendary character because
   A. the novel is gruesome
   B. the novel sheds light on the lead character's charismatic presence
   C. its author despises mythic tales
   D. Palahniuk is himself very prominent

Solution: The word "implies" tells us that the answer might not be directly stated. So do we freak out? It's too hard for us? No sir, ACT Crashers Rule #16: "Don't look for problems, make answers!" Stay focused. Don't overthink it. The answer will be very close to something that's actually stated. First, how do we know where to look? Examine your circled key words or scan the passage to find where *Rant* was introduced and discussed—the end of the second paragraph and the beginning of the third paragraph. Then use the process of elimination:

A. ~~the novel is gruesome~~—He does say that it's gruesome, but not relating to the legendary character.
B. ~~the novel sheds light on the lead character's charismatic presence~~—True, the novel is about a charismatic character, but that does not make it appropriate, it only restates the question.
C. ~~its author despises mythic tales~~—The passage never says he despises (hates) anything.
D. Palahniuk is himself very prominent—Yes, after stating that Palahniuk has achieved legendary status, the author states that it is "thusly apropos (fitting)" for his novel to be about a legendary character.

Correct answer: D

ACT Mantra #21
For "suggest" questions look for the answer that is hinted at in the passage;
though it might have different language, it should be pretty close to what is
actually said.

What Are You Trying to "Suggest"? Drills

Read the passage for main idea and tone, not to memorize details. We'll come back for those. Circle themes as you notice them. Also, if you come to a crazy-hard sentence, don't reread, move on. It's very liberating!

SOCIAL SCIENCE: This passage is adapted from "Emergent Democracies, Liberal Economic Policy: Pakistan and the Zakaria Hypothesis," an essay by Michael Brooks. Mohammed Ali Jinnah founded the nation of Pakistan.

An essential understanding of Pakistan's political history starts with an understanding of the motivations of the nation's founder Mohammed Ali Jinnah. As a politician, Jinnah
5 was a highly westernized and not a particularly religious man who was a leading figure in the Indian Independence movement.

In founding Pakistan, Jinnah sought protective space for the Subcontinent's minority Muslim
10 population and was interested in promoting western secular government as a base for Pakistan. While Pakistan was consciously Muslim in that its national identity was based on the independence and protection of
15 Muslims, the country did not, in Jinnah's vision, seek to impose an Islamic style of governing.

In fact, Jinnah sought to assure Pakistan's minorities that they would be protected and
20 allowed to worship freely. According to the biographical account, *Jinnah, Pakistan and Islamic Identity,* Jinnah espoused that Islamic teachings emphasize personal piety and universal tolerance, and that "western style
25 democracy," despite its flaws, was "the best system available to Muslims." It is safe to assert that Jinnah sought a state Islamic ethic and western style judicial and political systems of governance.

1. It can reasonably be inferred from the second paragraph that at the time when Mohammed Ali Jinnah founded Pakistan, Jinnah felt that the Muslim population on the subcontinent

   (A) was highly Westernized
   (B) was being ill-treated
   (C) was protective of their Indian heritage
   (D) did not want an independent state

2. By his statement "Islamic teachings . . . tolerance" in lines 23 and 24, the author is most nearly suggesting that Jinnah

   (F) believed that piety and tolerance are incompatible
   (G) thought that Islam could not function in a "western style democracy"
   (H) considered religious freedom important in Pakistan
   (J) sought to bring individual and state goals into harmony

3. It can most reasonably be inferred from the passage that when the author says "the motivations of the nation's founder" (line 3), he is most nearly referring to

   (A) Jinnah's desire for an Islamic government in Pakistan
   (B) Jinnah's hesitance to leave India
   (C) Jinnah's plan for a secular government in Pakistan
   (D) Jinnah's plan for a free India

Some Attitude

Remember from Skill 18 that as you read each passage, you are keeping in mind, "What is the main idea, and what is the author's attitude?" In this skill you will become an attitude master.

An author's attitude is expressed through choice of words and punctuation. For example, what is the attitude expressed in each of the following?

Ⓐ Politicians have once again overlooked the need for improvement in the infrastructure.
Attitude toward politicians: disapproval

Ⓑ Overworked politicians cannot be expected to foresee every need of their community.
Attitude toward politicians: compassion, forgiveness

Ⓐ Will Farrell is one funny guy.
Attitude toward Will Farrell: admiration, appreciation

Ⓑ You're such a "funny" guy.
Attitude: criticism, sarcasm

Remember to answer attitude questions based on evidence in the passage, not your own attitude toward the subject or outside knowledge. If you need help, try rereading the first and last lines of each paragraph. Often, these lines convey the author's attitude.

The ACT favors mellow attitudes. An extreme answer with all-out hatred or complete unqualified worship is not usually correct. Usually the answer is more moderate.

Let's take a look at the question from the Pretest.

22. In terms of mood, which of the following best describes the passage?
   F. Informative and sober
   G. Cautious but hopeful
   H. Distraught
   J. Apologetic and resolute

Solution: When you read a passage for main idea and tone, you essentially predict this question. For additional help you can reread the bold intro and the first and last sentences of the paragraphs. The author is giving a fairly unbiased (neutral) analysis of the decline and possible rebirth of Meadville's Main Street district. Let's use the process of elimination:

F. Informative and sober—Maybe, the passage is **informative** and **serious**.
G. ~~Cautious but hopeful~~—Though the passage does end with some **hope**, it is <u>not</u> **cautious**.
H. ~~Distraught~~—No, the passage is a serious analysis; it is not **emotional**.
J. ~~Apologetic and resolute~~—No, there is no **apology**.

Correct answer: F

ACT Mantra #22
Answer "attitude" questions based on evidence in the passage; an author's attitude is expressed through choice of words and punctuation. For help, reread the bold intro and the first and last sentences of each paragraph.

Some Attitude Drills

I'd left Santa Cruz earlier that morning, navigating the serpentine junctions of Highway 9, Highway 17, and Highway 1, and headed south toward Watsonville. I couldn't help but
5 feel irritated by the ongoing construction project to widen the highway. The towering red and yellow cranes, the pounding and clanging jackhammers, the blinding welders' torches, and orange safety barrel after orange safety barrel.
10 Finally, after a grueling mile or two, the traffic speed picked up, and I was freed from the city.

❶ How does the mood change in lines 10 and 11?

   Ⓐ From tension to fear

   Ⓑ From frustration to relief

   Ⓒ From irritation to haste

   Ⓓ From humor to anger

It is 60 years ago and you are at the "roof-top of the world," Tibet. You live peacefully, working to support your loved ones and contribute to your community. You live a life of quiet tradition in harmony with your surroundings. Non violence and prayer are cornerstones in your life as well as devotion to the leader, who you see not only as a political leader but as a spiritual leader as well. And then it happens; the peace is shattered as troops invade.

❷ Which of the following best describes the author's feelings about life before troops invaded?

   Ⓕ Pleasure lessened by fear

   Ⓖ Enjoyment mixed with guilt

   Ⓗ Reverence

   Ⓙ Suspicion

The conventional model for the criminal justice system is one of punishment: you break the law and you are punished, whether you pay with money, time, or your life. But, many forward-thinking prison officials, having seen from the inside that this approach doesn't work, have been asking themselves and those around them, "What can we do differently?"

❸ Which of the following best describes the prison officials' opinion about the conventional criminal justice system?

   Ⓐ Disregard and apathy

   Ⓑ Acknowledgment of the need for reform

   Ⓒ Respect for the institution

   Ⓓ Suspicion of foul play

The nervous system is complex in structure and equally complex in operation. The purpose of our experiment was to investigate various aspects of nervous responses and neural phenomena. This was achieved using two models of study. The generation of a nerve impulse and its response to stimulus was closely examined in the sciatic nerve of *Rana pipiens*. The same nerve-response loop was also observed on a computer simulator.

❹ In terms of mood, which of the following best describes the passage?

   Ⓕ Apologetic

   Ⓖ Hostile yet regretful

   Ⓗ Growing tension

   Ⓙ Instructive

Main Idea

A main idea is the general topic of a passage, what it's trying to get across. It answers the question, "So, what's your point?" That's the question that you kept in mind as you read the passage. Reading with this question in mind helps you

- stay focused;
- avoid getting caught up in memorizing details;
- gather an answer for the "main idea" question.

After you have answered all the detail and line number questions, go back to main idea and tone questions. Why wait? Because by the time you have completed the other questions, you have reread and rethought the passage, and you have an even better understanding of the main idea and tone.

Also, remember the bold intro. I showed you in Skill 17 that sometimes the bold intro actually gives away the main idea. And if you need more help, reread the first and last lines of each paragraph for clues to main idea.

Here's the question from the Pretest.

23. The main purpose of the passage can best be described as an effort to
   A. explain the appeal of American Main Streets
   B. explore the reasons for Meadville's struggling Main Street district
   C. examine contributing causes to the loss of Meadville's railroad infrastructure
   D. describe how Meadville's downtown has changed over the years

---

Solution: The title of the article given in the bold intro ("An Analysis of Meadville's Struggling Main Street District") actually gives this one away. I love this strategy; so many kids don't read the intro, but once you do, it helps so much! So the intro and the first and last lines in the paragraphs tell us that the passage is primarily about choice B, exploring the reasons for Meadville's struggling Main Street district. Don't get thrown by a wrong answer that contains words from the passage. Stay confident. Kids sometimes think, "Wow, that sounds nice; I don't get it, but it must be right." No! The right answer should make sense to you. It should fit the evidence in the passage.

Correct answer: B

ACT Mantra #23
If you need help with a "main idea" question, reread the bold intro and the first and last lines of each paragraph.

Main Idea Drills

Olmsted foresaw the need for plans at a time when they were considered mysterious. He anticipated that city parks would ensure future prosperity for the cities by increasing the value of city real estate, as well as creating a more balanced and egalitarian life for city dwellers then and in the future. Olmsted possessed an ability to see into the future and address future needs of city dwellers in his planning. In this way, his planning had a permanent effect on history that remains pertinent to our modern lifestyles. Even today, his concepts of city parks and landscaping are widely accepted and practiced.

1 The main point of the paragraph is that

Ⓐ city parks are essential to city real estate

Ⓑ Olmsted was a man of vision

Ⓒ city park planning has not changed much since Olmsted's time

Ⓓ Olmsted sought egalitarian city park use

During the tower's construction many Parisian citizens complained about the tower's aesthetics, inconvenience, and potential danger. Some people went so far as to testify in court. A number of well-known artists and musicians got together to sign a petition against the tower. They stated that it was ugly, useless, costly, and likely to fall in harsh weather. Gustave replied to the complaints by saying that he was as dedicated to the tower's aesthetics as they were and that he designed the tower in such a way that the iron lattice work created almost no wind resistance, thus ensuring the tower's endurance.

2 The main theme of this passage concerns

Ⓕ the controversy between residents of Paris and the tower's designer

Ⓖ the inconvenience and danger posed by the tower

Ⓗ the instability of the tower in harsh weather

Ⓙ Gustave's petition against the tower

Ma makes sassafras tea while Pa's boss compliments the tree. Then, they all sit down for grown-up talk while we gather round the tree to shake the copious presents. When carolers come by, we witness the enchanted looks on their faces as they too are inebriated by the magic of the gorgeous tree. Then Ma gives them some gingerbread and cider. If we had a tree like this, we'd never travel to Brooklyn to see Grandma; she'd come to us, despite the fact that she hates our dogs.

3 The passage is best described as

Ⓐ an illustration of a lasting relationship

Ⓑ a nostalgic recollection

Ⓒ a pleasant fantasy

Ⓓ an introduction to a character through another's eyes

Skill 24

Gretchen Is "Such" a Good Friend

And you know she cheats on Aaron? Yes, every Thursday he thinks she's doing SAT prep, but really she's hooking up with Shane Oman in the projection room above the auditorium! I never told anybody that because I am "such" a good friend!

Gretchen, *Mean Girls* (Paramount Pictures, 2004)

Why are there quote marks around "such"? In this example, it's to show that the word is emphasized. The ACT loves to ask questions like this—questions about why the author chose a certain word, punctuation mark, or method of developing a passage. These questions ask about the writer's choices and how a word functions, rather than solely about the main idea or what a word means.

Let's look at the question from the Pretest.

24. Which of the following statements best describes the structure of this passage?
   F. It contains a highly detailed anecdote that the author uses to prove a point.
   G. It presents logical analysis of the root causes of the economic hardships of Meadville's Main Street.
   H. It compares and contrasts the two major reasons for the economic difficulties of Meadville's Main Street.
   J. It begins with an impassioned plea for help and ends with encouraging news.

Solution: Review the structure of the passage, looking at the flow of how the paragraphs progress. Then use the process of elimination. Only eliminate an answer choice when you are **sure** that it doesn't work. Then choose the best from what's left. The passage does not give a **highly detailed anecdote** (story), **compare and contrast reasons**, or **make an impassioned plea** (request). It gives a step-by-step **logical analysis** of the causes of Meadville's problem.

Correct answer: G

ACT Mantra #24
For questions that ask about the writer's choices or the flow of the passage, review the progression of paragraphs and use the process of elimination.

Gretchen Is "Such" a Good Friend Drills

PROSE FICTION: This passage is adapted from the novel *Down the Bend* by David Rice.

Would we find Dan? I met Jules at the airport when I arrived, and we took a bus into the city. The specter of meeting Dan hung over my head those first three days, as did the fact that Mike,
5   our fourth friend, had neglected to apply for a visa and would consequently be unable to come at all.

I didn't wholeheartedly believe that we'd ever find Dan, but, on the third day, we set out from
10 the hostel in the direction of the Opera House and its grand surrounding square. It was Easter day and *even* the Amazon tour agencies appeared to be closed.

Circling around and around the Opera, slipping
15 on the slick cobblestones and looking at the shuttered-up bars and barbecue restaurants, we passed a soldier more than once, as he made rounds from his kiosk to the cathedral across from the Opera, and back.

20 Each time he saw us, he asked what we were doing, and Jules replied that we were looking for our friend. He didn't seem to think that was too good an idea, but he didn't say anything. He just nodded and resolved to ask the same
25 question next time he saw us.

On our way back to the hostel, having more or less given up, we were tired and noticed a small bakery that looked open. Just as it was starting to downpour, we ducked under the awning, and
30 then went inside. On the far right, under a TV in a wire cage, sat Dan, at a table with what looked like the family that owned the bakery, his bags piled up around his feet. He wore his winter jacket and it looked oddly appropriate,
35 soaked with tropical rain. The family smiled and brought us a platter of cinnamon rolls, pulling up two extra chairs.

1. In terms of developing the narrative, the third and fourth paragraphs (lines 14 to 25) primarily serve to

   (A) describe specific details of the Opera House to lend setting to the story
   (B) give a feeing of repetition and monotony in the search for Dan
   (C) portray the soldier in order to establish the contrast between him and Dan
   (D) depict the economic condition of the Opera House district

2. The author italicizes the word "even" in line 12 most likely to emphasize that

   (F) the agencies keep unpredictable hours
   (G) some people might want to take tours on a holiday
   (H) he is concerned about the credibility of the agencies' policies
   (J) if the tour companies were closed, then every business would be closed

3. The passage opens by posing a question that the passage

   (A) ponders
   (B) debates
   (C) answers
   (D) restates

4. In terms of the passage as a whole, the main function of the final paragraph is to

   (F) detail the unexpected way that they found Dan
   (G) introduce the owners of the bakery
   (H) criticize Dan's irresponsibility
   (J) conclude with a new set of questions to be answered in further paragraphs

Superbad Vocab I

The larger your vocabulary, the easier the passages will be to read and understand. Plus, several questions per test ask for the meaning of a word or phrase. Do you need to go out and memorize 1,000 new words? That'd be fine. But when you don't know the meaning of a word, you can also vibe it out. "Vibe it out" means that for words that you're not sure of, you can break them apart or consider where you might have seen or heard them used. You already know a lot more words than you might realize, even if you have not memorized their definitions.

Breaking Words

Many words in English break apart. For example, "circumnavigate" is a tough ACT word that most people don't know. But, "circum" means "around," like the circumference of a circle, and "navigate" just means "travel" or "plan a route." Thus, "circumnavigate" means to travel or plan a route around something. Breaking a word might get you an exact definition, or at least it will get you close enough to understand the word in context.

Superbad Vocabulary

To build your vocab, you can also use what's already in front of you, like movies. Here's a great example from the movie *Juno* (Fox Searchlight Pictures, 2007):

<u>Juno</u>: No, this is not a food baby all right? I've taken like three pregnancy tests, and I'm forshizz up the spout.
<u>Leah</u>: How did you even generate enough pee for three pregnancy tests? That's amazing. . . .
<u>Juno</u>: I don't know, I drank like, ten tons of Sunny D. . . . Anyway dude, I'm telling you I'm pregnant and you're acting shockingly **cavalier**.

What did Juno mean by "cavalier"? You can get it from the words around it. Juno is telling Leah that she's pregnant, which she is clearly upset about, and Leah doubts it and jokes around. Then Juno calls Leah "cavalier," so it must mean something like "too jokey" or "doubtful" or "not getting the seriousness here." And it does; "cavalier" means "too casual." Obviously, you might not memorize every new vocab word that comes at you while you munch popcorn, but if you keep your ears open, you'll pick up some of them.

Let's use this on the question from the Pretest.

25. The phrase "loss of major railroad infrastructure," as it is used in lines 6 and 7, most specifically refers to
   A. declines in profits of the railroad sector
   B. sizable delays experienced by trains traveling through Meadville
   C. decline of railroad use and facilities in Meadville
   D. lack of shopping happening in Meadville

Solution: You can answer this question by reading several lines after the phrase to find evidence of what it refers to, and you can also break apart the word "infrastructure" to make sure you've got it correct. "Infra" means "below" and "structure" just means "structure." So "infrastructure" means "the structure below," which is perfect and means "the organization or facilities of a system."

Correct answer: C

Superbad Vocab I Drills

Breaking Words

Use a dictionary to define the words in each group, and then conclude what the word parts must mean.

1 philanthropy _____   philosophy _____
technophile _____   technophobe _____
technology _____   phobia _____

"phil" means _____   "anthro" means _____
"soph" means _____   "tech" means _____
"phobe" means _____   "ology" means _____

2 homogeneous _____   heterogeneous _____
homosexual _____   heterosexual _____

"homo" means _____   "hetero" means _____
"gen" means _____

3 circumscribe _____   circumnavigate _____
circumvent _____   recirculate _____
transcribe _____   circumambulate _____

"circum" means _____   "scribe" means _____
"re" means _____   "trans" means _____

4 infrasonic _____   infraorder _____
"infra" means _____   "sonic" means _____

Movies

I'll give a quote from a movie, and you try to identify the movie and create an approximate definition for each **bold** ACT vocabulary word.

5 Elizabeth: Captain Barbossa, I am here to negotiate the **cessation** of **hostilities** against Port Royal.
Barbossa: There are a lot of long words in there, Miss; we're naught but humble pirates. What is it that you want?
Elizabeth: I want you to leave and never come back.
Barbossa: I'm **disinclined** to **acquiesce** to your request. Means "no."

Movie _____

"Cessation" means _____

"Hostilities" means _____

"Disinclined" means _____

"Acquiesce" means _____

6 Dennis: Oh, king eh? Very nice. And how'd you get that, eh? By **exploiting** the workers. By hanging on to outdated **imperialist dogma** which **perpetuates** the economic and social differences in our society. . . . Come to see the violence **inherent** in the system! I'm being repressed!

Movie _____

"Exploiting" means _____

"Imperialist" means _____

"Dogma" means _____

"Perpetuates" means _____

"Inherent" means _____

Superbad Vocab II

Word Associations

I remember when I was 17, the word "panache" showed up on a test. I didn't know the word, but I remembered that there was a fancy restaurant near my town called *Café Panache*. I thought, "What is Panache?" Obviously this fancy restaurant is not called *Café Smells Bad* or *Café I Hate You*. Some cafés might be called those names, but they are not the places my parents go. So, it must be *Café Delicious* or *Café Exciting* or *Café Good Times*. That insight was enough to vibe the word and get the question right. In fact, "panache" is similar to "exciting," it means "flair."

You can use anything around you to vibe out ACT vocab words. "Imperious" is a word that stumps most kids. But you've definitely seen it around. You've heard of "Imperial Stormtroopers" or an "Imperial Cruiser" in *Star Wars* and the "Imperious Curse" in *Harry Potter*. From these references you can certainly conclude that imperious must mean something like "big" or "grand" or "important," and that's enough to get an ACT question right. "Imperious" actually means "domineering, bossy, or authoritative." It makes sense that, in *Star Wars*, the Empire would have an Imperial Cruiser or that J. K. Rowling would use the word to describe a curse that gives control over another person!

So when you don't know a word or aren't sure of its definition, see if you can remember seeing or hearing the word anywhere—a billboard, a TV commercial, history class, Spanish class, *Harry Potter*, a restaurant name, a comic book, or *Magic: The Gathering* cards. Use anything that you can to figure it out.

Here's the question from the Pretest.

26. As it is used in line 16, the word "hastened" means
    F. slowed
    G. sped up
    H. stalled
    J. improved

Solution: The line states that "the lack of tourists **hastened** the decline of downtown," and then the sentence continues that "traveling Americans **rapidly** had fewer and fewer reasons to pass through Meadville." So, "hastened" means "made more rapid" or "sped up."

Correct answer: G

ACT Mantra #26
If you don't know the meaning of a word, ask yourself if you can break it apart or if you've heard or seen it in a book, in a movie, on a sign, as the name of a business, in a commercial, in a class, etc.

Superbad Vocab II Drills

Here are some great ACT vocab words. Let's see if you can vibe them out. Even if you can't define them, try to come up with an association. The goal here is not just for you to learn 13 new ACT words, but for you to become awake to all the great vocabulary that surrounds you.

Spanish

❶ "Diverting" might mean _____

❷ "Facile" might mean _____

French

❸ "Luminance" might mean _____

❹ "Clairvoyant" might mean _____

❺ "Comportment" might mean _____

❻ "Filial" might mean _____

The Grocery Store

❼ "Arid" might mean _____

Harry Potter

J. K. Rowling based the names of most charms and curses on English or Latin word parts. This is a font of ACT vocab; check out Wikipedia's entry for "Spells in Harry Potter."

❽ "Impervious" might mean _____

❾ "Stupefy" might mean _____

❿ "Conflagration" might mean _____

Dungeons and Dragons

All right, fess up and roll me a D20. *D&D* is a treasure chest of amazing ACT vocab words.

⓫ "Sagacious" might mean _____

⓬ "Haste" might mean _____

⓭ "Expeditious" might mean _____

Say What?

I told you that the correct answer will usually be a paraphrase of something directly stated in the passage. Sometimes they ask you to do the paraphrasing. They might ask, "Which of the following paraphrases line 31?" or "The author's reaction to _____ would most likely be . . . "

Let's take a look at this on the Pretest.

27. According to the last paragraph, which of the following statements would the author most likely make with regard to Meadville?
   A. While Meadville's downtown had struggled, it has come a long way and is quickly recovering.
   B. While Meadville's downtown has struggled, there are possibilities for recovery.
   C. Meadville's downtown had struggled until it was revived by the Main Street Project.
   D. Meadville's struggles have taught the business community valuable lessons that will lead to future economic growth.

Solution: The author stated in the last paragraph that Meadville is receiving funding from the Main Street Project to help improve downtown and that Meadville has many positive qualities such as being beautiful, historic, home to a college, and near a highway. These are all factors that could help Meadville recover, so choice B is correct. The paragraph does not state that Meadville "is quickly recovering," or that it "has been revived" already, or that "valuable lessons" have been learned.

Correct answer: B

ACT Mantra #27
For a "Say what?" question, don't get thrown if the choices are not from the passage. Stay relaxed and focused, and look for the choice that answers the specific goal of the question.

Say What? Drills

SOCIAL SCIENCE: This passage is adopted from the essay "Derrida and Levi-Strauss" by David Rice. Jacques Derrida was a philosopher who lived from 1930 to 2004. Claude Levi-Strauss is a French social anthropologist.

Jacques Derrida's aim in *Structure, Sign, and Play in the Discourse of the Human Sciences* (1978), was not to reveal or explicate something true, or even reasonable, but to put on a
5 performance, a play, a series of elaborate and intriguing games which ruminate on the mind's inability either to think without imagining a center or to believe that one exists.

Claude Levi-Strauss revealed a series of
10 elemental contradictions while plumbing the depths of mythic thought, hoping to arrange his findings coherently, as his *Overture to The Raw and the Cooked* (1964) promised, but he tried to work *through* or *past* them. Derrida, revisiting
15 these contradictions, works *with* them, celebrating rather than trying to resolve their tension. Thus the most salient difference between structuralism and poststructuralism is a greater sense of self-importance in the prior,
20 and a greater sense of self-deprecating humor in the latter.

As a poststructuralist, Derrida criticized Levi-Strauss in order to criticize himself and his ambiguous position as an intellectual in an age
25 that both demands and disdains intellectualism, miring in a struggle to get beyond language while growing ever more certain that language is all there is.

❶ Which of the following questions is NOT answered in the passage?

  Ⓐ Has Levi-Strauss published his ideas?

  Ⓑ What is a difference between Derrida and Levi-Strauss?

  Ⓒ Has Derrida commented on Levi-Strauss' writings?

  Ⓓ What languages has Derrida learned?

❷ According to the first paragraph, which of the following statements would the author most likely make with regard to Derrida?

  Ⓕ Derrida sought absolute truth.

  Ⓖ Derrida sought clear understanding.

  Ⓗ Derrida sought to explore.

  Ⓙ Thinking was difficult for Derrida.

❸ Which of the following statements best paraphrases lines 14 to 17 ("Derrida revisiting . . . tension.")?

  Ⓐ Whereas Derrida embraced flawed reality, Levi-Strauss tried to fix it.

  Ⓑ Levi-Strauss missed the point and Derrida got it.

  Ⓒ Contradictions bothered Derrida more than they bothered Levi-Strauss.

  Ⓓ Resolution was more important to Derrida than it was to Levi-Strauss.

❹ The contrast between accepting and trying to change something is best exemplified by which of the following quotations from the passage?

  Ⓕ "reveal or explicate something true"

  Ⓖ "think without imagining"

  Ⓗ "celebrating rather than trying to resolve"

  Ⓙ "demands and disdains intellectualism"

How to Read

Sometimes ACT passages are obscenely dense and kids panic, "I can't do it! It'll take too long. It'll kill me." Relax, and remember your Skills. Read the passage, looking for main idea and tone. Don't memorize details. Don't reread a confusing line. Don't reread if you spaced out and missed a sentence or two. There's no single sentence or even paragraph that you need to get the main idea and tone. And for details, you'll reread the lines later anyway.

All this will save you time and energy. Remember my story from Skill 18. When I was 16 years old and preparing for standardized tests, I did well in school but didn't read much. I was terrified. Then one day I was like, "Wait, this is ridiculous, how long can it take?" So I took out a stopwatch and timed myself. It took 3 minutes! Try it, and you'll see. Even for a slow reader, the passage takes only a few minutes, especially if you use the Skills.

So read the following huge passage. Read quickly but stay relaxed. Pretend you love the topic. As you read, ask yourself, What are the main idea and tone? Use all the Skills. Time yourself. You'll see that even a ridiculously long passage takes only a few minutes.

Here's the Pretest question.

28. Which of the following does the author cite as a reason why people do not shop in downtown Meadville?
  F. It is far from another city.
  G. It has no significant Main Street.
  H. The county's residents have the money to shop at other, more expensive stores.
  J. Meadville's rural location draws them away from downtown.

Solution: Refer to your circled key words or scan the passage for a reason why people do not shop in downtown Meadville. The third paragraph cites the fact that "Meadville is 45 minutes from any major metropolis" as a reason for the lack of shoppers. The passage does not state that Meadville has no significant Main Street, that the residents are wealthy (it says they are poor), or that the rural location draws them from downtown (which makes no sense if you think about it).

Correct answer: F

> **ACT Mantra #28**
> **Read the passage, looking for main idea and tone. Don't memorize details.**
> **Don't reread a confusing line. Don't reread if you spaced out and missed a**
> **sentence or two.**

How to Read Drills

Directions: Read the passage below. Look for main idea and tone. Don't memorize details. Circle themes as you notice them. Time yourself. Then look at the Solutions page.

HUMANITIES: This passage is adopted from Richard Wylde's essay "The Case for Vulgarity."

There is a fine difference between vulgarity used as a part of the artistic process and vulgarity for the sheer experience of shock. To be of any worth whatsoever, vulgarity cannot be a work's only drawing aspect. Vulgarity for vulgarity's sake is exploitation, which may equal high entertainment value, but exploitation art has little to no artistic merit.

To say that vulgarity in art is simply a representation of real life, or that it is holding a mirror up to society and showing us our own depravity is an old, tired argument. Despite the possible corruption of our children and ourselves, vulgarity is clearly here to stay and it is clear that the population at large likes it.

But then again, is that really vulgarity? Going back to the definition of vulgarity, which is simply anything that offends traditional values, it seems that the concepts and presentations of swearing, violence, and sex are not all that taboo anymore. To truly be considered vulgar today, one would have to go to some lengths, but that only really produces the sensation of shock. And, if shocking the audience is the artist's main goal, probably their piece is lacking in some other meaningful aspect.

Why vulgarity? Do we enjoy the grotesque and unusual? Carl Jung teaches that each of us has a pleasant self with which we identify, called the ego, and a hidden self which we each tend to reject and deny, which he called our "shadow." "The shadow" points to our guilty pleasures for things like violence, which we know are wrong, but we still take a perverse enjoyment in viewing.

Perhaps there is safeness in being the voyeur, because it appeals to our dark side without making us culpable. For instance, I like zombie movies. But if I were to be given a questionnaire asking "Do you like to see people's heads being blown off with a shotgun?" I would be disgusted and deny it. Yet judging by my viewing habits, I *do* like it!

While the shadow is part of who we are, we deny or fear its existence. No one would say they like to see someone stabbed with a knife, yet this is a very common incident in horror movies. We can make up all the explanations we want about the thrill of fear, but all signs seem to point to a complex where, on a deep unconscious level, we like to see other people stabbed with knives. Perhaps knowing that the violence is not real and that we are simply observers waiting to have our senses aroused, we feel okay about the pleasure.

Vulgarity makes the abstract idea of "conflict" something concrete and brings it directly to the senses. It makes us sit up and pay attention, because something in our environment is not right, not in harmony with its surroundings. This works much the same way that dissonance functions in music. Tones that don't sound "correct" have a way of grabbing our attention more so than "complete-sounding" chords. When the resolution finally comes, the sense of opposition is "solved," and makes our appreciation for normal musical consonance that much greater. It seems sweeter.

Vulgarity is discord, briefly jarring our concept of what is acceptable. Having a few images or descriptions of real ugliness makes everything else that much more beautiful. Of course there's no formula, and constant vulgarity is an overstimulation, but the point is that vulgarity needn't be just for demented entertainment value. It creates a defiant mood that can either be built on or be left to wallow in its own filth.

How to Be a Reading Ninja

You've now learned the 12 Reading Skills that you need for the ACT. The Mantras remind you what to do for each type of question. Let's make sure you've memorized them. Drill them until you are ready to teach them. Then do that; find a willing friend and give a little ACT course.

Learning the Mantras is like learning martial arts. Practice until they become part of you—until you follow them naturally: when you see a passage, you read for main idea and tone, and when you answer questions, you recognize most question types and know what to do. This will definitely raise your score. It might even fundamentally change you as a student. After ACT prep many students have better study habits. They read the intros in their history books, they read faster and with better comprehension, they are able to anticipate quiz questions. Homework becomes less intimidating, easier, and more fun. So, good work; your ACT score and probably even your school grades will go up!

Here are the 12 ACT Reading Mantras. Check the box next to each Skill when you have mastered it. Reread the Skill sections if you need to.

☐ **Skill 17.** Always begin a reading passage by reading the bold intro.

☐ **Skill 18.** Read the passage, looking for main idea and tone. That helps you stay focused; keep asking yourself, What are the main idea and tone? When you notice the theme of a paragraph, circle a word or words that capture it. Don't try to memorize details and don't reread hard lines. If you need them, you'll reread later when you know the question and what to look for.

☐ **Skill 19.** To answer a "most nearly means" question, reread a few lines before and a few lines after.

☐ **Skill 20.** For a "direct info" question, always read before and after a line or key word and find proof.

☐ **Skill 21.** For "suggest" questions look for the answer that is hinted at in the passage; though it might have different language, it should be pretty close to what is actually said.

☐ **Skill 22.** Answer "attitude" questions based on evidence in the passage; an author's attitude is expressed through choice of words and punctuation. For help, reread the bold intro and the first and last sentences of each paragraph.

☐ **Skill 23.** If you need help with a "main idea" question, reread the bold intro and the first and last lines of each paragraph.

☐ **Skill 24.** For questions that ask about the writer's choices or the flow of the passage, review the progression of paragraphs and use the process of elimination.

☐ **Skills 25 and 26.** If you don't know the meaning of a word, ask yourself if you can break it apart, or if you've ever heard or seen it in a book, in a movie, on a sign, as the name of a business, in a commercial, in a class, etc.

☐ **Skill 27.** For a "Say what?" question, don't get thrown if the choices are not from the passage. Stay relaxed and focused, and look for the choice that answers the specific goal of the question.

76

☐ **Skill 28.** Read the passage, looking for main idea and tone. Don't memorize details. Don't reread a confusing line. Don't reread if you spaced out and missed a sentence or two.

Here's the question from the Pretest.

29. Which of the following best describes the author's tone in the final sentence of the passage?
    A. Angry but regretful
    B. Ironic
    C. Sullen but resolved
    D. Apologetic

Solution: The final sentence states, "It's also, both fortunately and unfortunately, a very inexpensive place to own a business," meaning that fortunately it's an inexpensive place to own a business, which is good, but it's also unfortunate because it's only inexpensive because it's not a thriving area. So the tone is ironic. You can also use the process of elimination. The author does not express anger or resolved sullenness (sulking and a sense of having accepted the problem—he has hope), and he does not apologize.

Correct answer: B

How to Avoid the Five Most Common Careless Errors on ACT Reading Questions

1. Don't choose an answer just because you recognize words from the passage. Often, the correct answer will paraphrase the passage rather than directly quote it.
2. Don't select an answer based on just the first few words; the whole answer should make sense.
3. Be mindful on EXCEPT and LEAST/MOST questions.
4. Find evidence for your answer; be a lawyer. Use evidence from the passage, not your own outside knowledge or opinions.
5. Don't get intimidated. If a question seems hard, look for the evidence, decide what type of question it is, use your Mantras, and remember ACT Crashers Rule #45: No excuses. Test like a champion!

How to Be a Reading Ninja Drills

Identify each question type, and then choose the best answer.

HUMANITIES: This passage is adapted from Manpriya Kaur Samra's essay "Mysticism and the Validity of Religious Experience: Cognitive Value and a Multiplicity of Verification."

Mysticism consists of provocative experiential claims, and though they may be considered outside the norm, these claims are accepted religious practice amongst and across faiths. A
5 revered poet across religions, cultures and traditions in South Asia, Kabir stood out as a radical in the philosophic climate of his time.

Fifteenth century northern India's political and philosophic atmosphere was shaped both by
10 beliefs of the ancient traditions of Brahminism and by the recent addition of Islam brought and practiced by the Mughal rulers. It was also determined by the woes of ethnic and religious conflict between the two.

15 Kabir did not identify himself as a Hindu or Muslim, nor as saint or guru. He simply assigned himself the status of a disciple, a man who lived simply in the material world to meditate upon the human spirit and its relation
20 to the divine.

Kabir's medium of song and oral poetry spread his name throughout society in the subcontinent. His poems eventually became scripture for a number of religious traditions:
25 the Bakhti mystic tradition, the Sufi Islamic tradition and the Sikh tradition. His ability and the ability of others in the mystic tradition to cut across ethnic, religious, philosophic and mundane socio-economic and lingual barriers
30 demonstrate their power to inspire.

---

1 The passage indicates that Kabir's poetry was used by

Ⓐ the Bakti tradition only

Ⓑ the Bakti, Sufi, and Sikh traditions

Ⓒ the Mughal rulers

Ⓓ people around the world

2 By "philosophical climate" (line 7), the author most nearly means

Ⓕ intellectual environment

Ⓖ stormy arguments

Ⓗ university gatherings

Ⓙ religious plans

3 According to the third paragraph, which of the following statements would the author most likely make with regard to Kabir?

Ⓐ Kabir sought to isolate himself.

Ⓑ Kabir sought clear understanding.

Ⓒ Kabir sought to overthrow the king.

Ⓓ Kabir is difficult to appreciate.

4 In terms of mood, which of the following best describes the passage?

Ⓕ Mysterious

Ⓖ Stirring

Ⓗ Provocative

Ⓙ Instructive

5 The author's main point about mysticism is that it is

Ⓐ philosophical

Ⓑ inspiring

Ⓒ confrontational

Ⓓ widely accepted

Clear the Mechanism: Meditation, Baseball, and the ACT

Life is a series of now points.
Sujata, *Beginning to See*

Ben finished the ACT math section and realized that he had made careless errors on at least two questions. He was hoping to break 32 and got upset. As he began the Reading section, he was flustered and had trouble focusing.

Realizing that he had made careless errors was very disappointing. But lamenting the careless errors did not help Ben; it only hurt his focus on the rest of the test. What could he have done? The answer lies in the wisdom of sage Kevin Costner, or at least in his character Billy Chapel from the baseball movie *For Love of the Game*.

In the movie Costner plays a veteran pitcher for the Tigers. He's a massive superstar with only 134 career losses during 18 seasons. On the mound Chapel is a samurai, impervious to distraction and pressure. How does he achieve this state? When he needs to focus, he stares at the catcher's glove and says, "Clear the mechanism." The noise of the crowd, the flashing lights, and the taunts of Yankee fans disappear, and Chapel enters the zone.

"Clear the mechanism" is Chapel's mantra to get focused. He tunes out distraction and focuses on only his movement, the pitch, the ball, and the catcher. He is present. He does not hear the jeers or cheers of the fans, and he rebounds instantly from a terrible pitch or botched play. Lamenting a bad pitch would in no way make the next one better. Each pitch comes from a fresh and clear head.

You can do this too. You don't have to say, "Clear the mechanism," although you can if you like. Instead, you can say, "I am focused," "I feel my feet," or "Asparagus." The phrase does not matter, except that after you have practiced saying it and then getting present enough times, the phrase will be a trigger, like it is for Chapel, to get present and tune out distractions.

How do you get good at it? The same way that you get good at most things: practice. Practice as often as you can remember. Do it in school, on the field, during band practice, at parties, and at the ACT. Anytime you think of it, say your phrase, and then feel your feet, notice sensations in your body, feel your breathing, notice your thoughts, and feel the pencil, ball, french fry, or tuba in your hand. Get present, focusing entirely on what you are doing, fully awake to sensations and thoughts of the moment.

Getting present is a high. And the more you practice, the better you'll be at it. Then if you're taking a test or you're on the field and something goes wrong, you can kick the dirt or bang your fist to let it out and then "Clear the mechanism," and completely move on, unburdened, unflustered, and ready to give the next moment 100% of your attention.

Five Tips for a Great College Application

I asked Heather Johnson, a private educational consultant in western Massachusetts, to give us her five most important college application tips. She said, "The single most important piece of advice is to start early and get organized. Then you can do your best and stress less, a pretty good tradeoff." Here's the rest of what she said:

❶ Take the most challenging high school courses that are available and appropriate for you.

❷ Meet your guidance counselors or college counselors as early as you can. Get to know them and establish a relationship so that they can provide more personalized guidance and write a more powerful letter of recommendation.

❸ If your colleges require the ACT or SAT, plan ahead. To maximize your score and dramatically reduce senior-year stress, begin preparing for and taking the test in the spring of 11th grade.

❹ Visit college campuses. Take advantage of long weekends and vacations during junior year to visit colleges while they are in session. You'll get the real feel for a school and its students; plus the earlier you visit schools, the earlier you'll be able to narrow down your list.

❺ Make a chart of the schools that you are applying to that includes requirements (standardized tests, teacher recommendations, essays, supplements, etc.) and due dates. Use the chart to plan ahead and complete applications before deadlines.

Science

> . . . that's why you and I don't see eye-to-eye sometimes, Jack, because you're a man of **science**.
>
> John Locke, *Lost* (ABC, 2004)

If you like science, this section will be easy for you. And if you don't like science, this section will be . . . easy for you, too. Here's the deal: there is nothing that you need to memorize from biology, chemistry, ecology, geology, physics, or any other science course for the ACT Science section. It only tests your ability to read tables and graphs. And it always asks the same six types of questions. Every time! Get comfortable with these six types of questions, and your score will go way up! Let's take a look.

How to Read Science

ACT Myth: You need to love science to ace the ACT Science section.

ACT Mythbusters: ACT Science is just reading comprehension of tables and graphs. So if you like science, reading, math, or even just checking the stats of your favorite Red Sox pitcher, you can read a table, and you've got it covered.

The most important ACT Science strategy is "Don't Be Intimidated." You won't be balancing chemical equations, converting grams to moles, calculating newtons of force, or classifying spiders into their proper phylum. You will just be reading tables and graphs. This should be no different from checking the stats on your high school bowling team or your favorite Wii high-scorer.

The second most important ACT Science strategy is: "Work Quickly." There are seven passages for you to do in 35 minutes—that's 5 minutes per passage. Can you do it? Yes! Here's how. Read the paragraphs quickly. Duh. No seriously, read quickly, not to memorize, and if they are very difficult, not even to understand, just to get the gist of what the whole experiment is generally about. Then glance at the graphs—just glance. Read the words and just note what they are about. This whole process of "reading" the science passage should take 20 to 30 seconds tops. Then go to the questions. Each question will tell you which table or graph to look back at anyway.

Let's look at the question from the Pretest.

30. Based on the data in Figure 2, at sites 1 and 2 the deposit of lowest copper concentration in the groundwater was recorded at a depth of
  F. 5 m
  G. 20 m
  H. 24 m
  J. 50 m

Solution: The question tells you exactly where to look for the answer. In both graphs of Figure 2, the lowest copper concentrations are at a depth of 20 m. The only way to get this question wrong is to get intimidated by the wording or by the weird explanation of the experiment. But the actual experiment rarely matters in an ACT science question; you'll mostly just use the tables and graphs. If the wording of a question is confusing, reread it a few times and then do the thing that seems most obvious. That's usually correct for ACT Science questions!

Correct answer: G

ACT Mantra #30
Read ACT Science passages quickly, just to get the gist of what the
experiment is generally about. Then glance at the graphs and
go to the questions.

How to Read Science Drills

Let's practice reading science passages. Remember to read quickly, **just** to get the gist of what the experiment is generally about. Then **glance** at the tables or graphs. See if you can read this entire science passage in under 30 seconds, and then answer the question, What is the passage generally about?

Passage I

The *total mechanical energy* (TME) of an object equals the sum of its *potential energy* (PE) and its *kinetic energy* (KE). An object's potential energy is given by the equation PE = *mgh*, where *m* is its mass, *h* is its height above a reference point, and *g* is the acceleration due to gravity (9.8 m/s²). The object's kinetic energy is given by the equation KE = *mv²*/2, where *v* is its velocity.

Velocity is defined as "the speed of an object in a given direction."

A student performed 2 experiments to investigate TME.

Experiment 1
Starting from rest at point *A*, Natalia pushed a 2.2 kg ball down a frictionless track in an airless vacuum chamber.

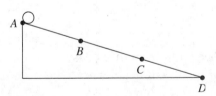

Figure 1

At various points along the incline, Natalia determined the ball's KE and PE in joules.

Table 1			
Position	Height (m)	KE (J)	PE (J)
A	12	0.0	258.7
B	8	86.2	172.5
C	4	172.5	86.2
D	0	258.7	0.0

Experiment 2
Natalia repeated the experiment on a non-frictionless track in a non-vacuum, that is, in air of ordinary atmospheric pressure. In all other ways, as much as possible, the track was identical to the track in Experiment 1.

At the same points along the incline, Natalia determined the ball's speed.

Table 2		
Position	Height (m)	Ball speed (m/s)
A	12	0.0
B	8	8.35
C	4	11.6
D	0	13.8

What is the passage generally about?

Skill 31

How to Read Tables and Graphs

You've read the paragraphs quickly, not to memorize them, and if they are very difficult, not even to understand them, just to get the gist of what the experiment is generally about. You've glanced at the tables and graphs. Next, do the questions. The most common ACT Science question asks you to find a value or a fact on a table or graph. And usually the question tells you exactly which table or graph to look back at!

Let's see this on the question from the Pretest.

31. According to Figure 1, which of the following has the thinnest deposit?
   A. Sand and gravel at site 1
   B. Sand and gravel at site 2
   C. Brown till at site 2
   D. Bedrock at site 1

Solution: The question tells us to look at Figure 1. If it doesn't tell you where to look, just scan the tables and graphs for the one that has the terms from the question. This question asks for the thinnest layer on the diagram. So, looking at Figure 1, try the answers and use the process of elimination.

A. Sand and gravel at site 1—Maybe, pretty thin.

B. ~~Sand and gravel at site 2~~—No, thicker than site 1.

C. ~~Brown till at site 2~~—Nope, thicker.

D. ~~Bedrock at site 1~~—No, thick.

Don't get intimidated by the question. Assume that it's asking something easy. Don't be afraid to look for something obvious. It literally wants the thinnest layer in the diagram.

Correct answer: A

ACT Mantra #31
The most common ACT Science question asks you to find a value or a fact from the tables or graphs. And usually the question tells you exactly which table or graph to look back at!

How to Read Tables and Graphs Drills

Let's practice the first type of ACT Science question: finding a value on a graph or table.

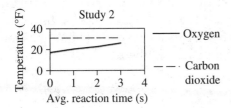

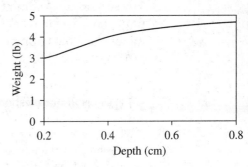

Figure 1

❶ Based on the average reaction times used in Study 2, compared with the corresponding temperature for oxygen, carbon dioxide has a temperature at a given average reaction time that is

Ⓐ always lower

Ⓑ always the same

Ⓒ always higher

Ⓓ sometimes lower and sometimes higher

❸ According to Figure 1, a rabbit footprint found 0.6 cm deep in wet loam soil would indicate that the rabbit weighed which of the following?

Ⓐ 2.5 lb

Ⓑ 3.5 lb

Ⓒ 4.5 lb

Ⓓ 5.5 lb

Experiment 1

Time (s)	Percent concentration in region 2
0	12.3
9	29.7
12	31.8
15	43.9

Experiment 2

	Rayon	Wool	Vinyl	Fiberglass
Heat retention	71%	82%	89%	92%
Linear expansion (mm)	0.91	0.84	0.95	0.12

❷ In Experiment 1, the *effusion time* of the gas was the time required for the gas to reach 20% concentration in region 2. The effusion time for the gas was

Ⓕ less than 9 s

Ⓖ between 9 and 12 s

Ⓗ between 12 and 15 s

Ⓙ greater than 15 s

❹ Based on the results of Experiment 2, if an engineer needs an insulation that retains over 90% heat, which of the following should she choose?

Ⓕ Rayon

Ⓖ Wool

Ⓗ Vinyl

Ⓙ Fiberglass

Up and Down

The second most common type of ACT Science question asks you to look at a chart or graph and decide what happens to one thing as another changes, like "as heat increases, what happens to volume?" This is just a specific type of Skill 31 question; you just have to read the graph. Every ACT test has several of these.

> Let's look at the question from the Pretest.
>
> **32.** According to Figure 1, as the thickness of the brown till deposit increases from site 1 to site 2, the thickness of the sand and gravel above it
>   **F.** increases
>   **G.** remains the same
>   **H.** decreases
>   **J.** first decreases then increases

Solution: Literally, look at Figure 1 and look at how thick the sand and gravel layer is from site 1 to site 2. As long as you stay focused, this is easy. Kids tend to miss this one when they are intimidated and think it must be harder than it is. In these Skills you will learn to expect every kind of ACT Science question. No surprises. From site 1 to site 2 the thickness of the sand and gravel layer, shown in white on the diagram, increases. You might think that it increases and then decreases, but that is not an answer choice anyway. Notice that choice J is incorrect because it says the opposite.

Correct answer: F

ACT Mantra #32
The second most common type of ACT Science question asks you to look at a chart or graph and decide what happens to one thing as another changes.

Up and Down Drills

Here are several of the same graphs from Skill 31, but with type II questions.

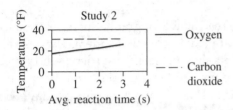

❶ Based on the average reaction times used in Study 2, one can conclude that as the average reaction time increases, the temperatures of the carbon dioxide and of oxygen do which of the following?

	Carbon dioxide	Oxygen
Ⓐ	Increase only	Increase only
Ⓑ	Increase only	Increase, then decrease
Ⓒ	Remain the same	Increase only
Ⓓ	Remain the same	Increase, then decrease

Experiment 1

Time (s)	Percent concentration in region 1
0	7.3
5	15.7
10	30.2
15	59.9

❷ Which of the following hypotheses about the relationship between time and percent concentration in region 1 is best supported by the data in Experiment 1? Every 5 seconds, percent concentration in region 1 approximately

Ⓕ halves

Ⓖ doubles

Ⓗ remains unchanged

Ⓙ sometimes halves and sometimes doubles

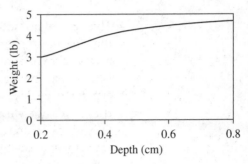

Figure 1

❸ According to Figure 1, if the same rabbit left a print 0.2 cm deep in the spring and 0.6 cm deep in the summer, then the rabbit's weight probably increased by

Ⓐ 0.5 lb

Ⓑ 1.0 lb

Ⓒ 1.5 lb

Ⓓ 4.5 lb

Experiment 2

	Rayon	Wool	Vinyl	Fiberglass
Heat retention	71%	82%	89%	92%
Linear expansion (mm)	0.91	0.84	0.95	0.12

❹ Based on the data in Experiment 2, the researchers should draw which of the following conclusions about the relationship between heat retention and linear expansion for the materials shown?

Ⓕ There is no noticeable relationship between heat retention and linear expansion.

Ⓖ As heat retention increases, linear expansion increases.

Ⓗ As heat retention increases, linear expansion decreases.

Ⓙ As heat retention decreases, linear expansion decreases.

Between the Lines

This type of question still asks you just to read a table or graph. But it asks you to use the table or graph to determine the value for a data point not shown. The answer is always above, below, or between the points shown; like if your friend who plays Tetris half an hour per day can get to level 8, and your friend who plays four hours per day can get to level 83, what level can Mikayla reach if she plays 2 hours per day? Seem tricky? It's not; we just want a number about halfway between 8 and 83, and they will only give you one number even remotely halfway between them! They will NEVER expect you to do much math. The key to this type of question is: don't get intimidated!

Let's see this on the question from the Pretest.

33. If a sample were taken at site 2 at a depth of 35 m, it would most likely show a copper concentration closest to
   A. 1.0 ppm
   B. 0.8 ppm
   C. 0.55 ppm
   D. 0.25 ppm`

Solution: This question does not tell us where to look. So just scan the figures for the one that gives copper concentration for site 2. Figure 1 does not give copper concentrations. Figure 2 does, and we want the second graph of Figure 2, for site 2. A sample with a depth of 35 m is not shown, but following the pattern of the data, it looks like a sample of 35 m would have a copper concentration of a little over 0.5%. Notice that the choices only give one answer even close to 0.5. They do this on purpose. When you have to estimate for this type of question, they will not try to fool you or expect you to do complex calculations to get the answer.

Correct answer: C

ACT Mantra #33
The third type of ACT Science question asks you to use the graph or table
to determine the value for a data point that is not shown, but is above, below,
or between points that are shown.

Between the Lines Drills

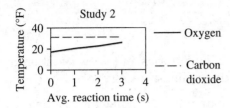

Study 2

1. According to Study 2, if the temperature for a certain gas was measured to be 19.5°F after an average reaction time of 0.5 s, we can conclude that

   (A) the gas is nitrogen
   (B) the gas is oxygen
   (C) the gas is carbon dioxide
   (D) the gas is helium

Experiment 1

Time (s)	Percent concentration in region 2
0	12.3
3	15.7
6	30.2
12	59.9

2. If the percent concentration were found to be 23%, the elapsed time would likely have been

   (F) 0 s
   (G) 2 s
   (H) 4 s
   (J) 7 s

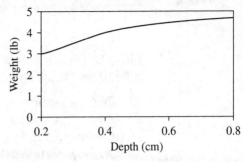

Figure 1

3. If the graph in Figure 1 were continued beyond the data shown, it would likely show that a 1.0 cm deep footprint would be left by a rabbit that weighs closest to

   (A) 3.5 lb
   (B) 4.0 lb
   (C) 5.0 lb
   (D) 9.0 lb

Experiment 2

	Rayon	Wool	Vinyl	Fiberglass
Heat retention	71%	82%	89%	92%
Linear expansion (mm)	0.91	0.84	0.95	0.12

4. If a fifth insulator is added to the table and has a heat retention factor of 77%, does the table support the conclusion that the fifth insulator should have a linear expansion factor of 0.87 mm?

   (F) Yes; since its heat retention is between rayon and wool, its linear expansion will be also.
   (G) Yes; since the heat retention is slightly above rayon's, the linear expansion will be slightly below.
   (H) No; the linear expansion would be 0.85.
   (J) No; heat retention does not predict linear expansion.

The Paragraphs

Most ACT science questions only use the tables and graphs. But a few questions per test refer to the paragraphs. These questions test three things:

❶ These questions might ask you about the paragraphs, just like the Reading section.
❷ They might be exactly like regular "read the graph" questions but use a term given in the paragraph in place of the one shown in the graph.
❸ Or, they might cite words and numbers from the paragraph that make the question seem complex but are actually unnecessary and just restating the conditions of the experiment.

We'll practice each of these in the drills. Basically, when you see a question that refers to a graph, but you don't see the terms from the question in the graph, look at the paragraphs.

Let's try this on the question from the Pretest.

34. Based on the data in Figure 2, the largest natural copper deposit most likely existed
   F. near the surface of site 1
   G. near the surface of site 2
   H. deep at site 1
   J. deep at site 2

Solution: Figure 2 pretty much gives us the answer. But we need the info from the paragraph to be sure. The paragraph stated that corroding natural copper deposit is one reason for elevated copper levels in groundwater. So the most likely place for a deposit would be the place of highest concentration. And according to Figure 2, deep in site 1 has the highest copper concentration that we know of. It has a value of over 1 ppm, which is higher than anywhere else in our data.

Correct answer: H

```
ACT Mantra #34
When you see a question that refers to a graph, but you don't see the terms
from the question in the graph, look at the paragraphs.
```

The Paragraphs Drills

A study was conducted to determine whether a salt/sand alternative proved effective on frozen road surfaces. Researchers predicted that a given amount of salt/sand mixture could be used interchangeably with ordinary road salt.

Ordinary road salt, composed primarily of NaCl, was compared with a 50% NaCl and 50% sand mixture. The salinity (salt concentration) of the road salt used in both was identical. The scientists gathered data from road crews in Dunnville, Ontario. The road crews reported the pounds of salt or salt/sand mixture needed for a 1-mile stretch of a two-lane road. The results are presented in the table.

Road surface temperature(°C)	NaCl (lb)	NaCl and sand (lb)	Application
>0	100	200	As needed
−4 to −1	200	400	As needed
−9 to −5	250	500	Every 2 h
−14 to −10	300	600	Every 2 h

❶ According to the study, when a mixture has 50% NaCl and 50% sand, the amount of this mixture needed versus the amount of NaCl needed for a 1-mile stretch of a two-lane road will be

Ⓐ double

Ⓑ equal

Ⓒ one-half

Ⓓ one-quarter

❷ Based on the data in the table, one can conclude that when the temperature of a road surface decreases, the amount of ordinary road salt needed

Ⓕ increases only

Ⓖ decreases only

Ⓗ increases, then decreases

Ⓙ remains the same

❸ Do the data in the table support the prediction proposed by the researchers?

Ⓐ Yes, since the amount of mixture increased at the same rate as the ordinary road salt.

Ⓑ Yes, since the amount of mixture needed was always double the amount of ordinary road salt needed.

Ⓒ No, since the amount of mixture needed was always double the amount of ordinary road salt needed.

Ⓓ No, since the amount needed for the mixture varied with different road surface temperatures.

❹ According to the data in the table, ordinary road salt was applied every 2 hours beginning at a road surface temperature of

Ⓕ −10°C

Ⓖ −9°C

Ⓗ −5°C

Ⓙ −4°C

Don't Be Controlled

This is the one type of question where they might ask you something even remotely sciency. I have seen two types of this question:

❶ **Commonsense questions.** The way to get these wrong is to assume you don't know the answer because you don't remember it from science class. The way to get it right is to just think it through and to use common sense and the process of elimination. For example, if stomach acid digests meat in the stomach, and the stomach acid must touch the meat to work, which of the following would improve digestion? The answer would be something like "chewing more" since that will break down the big chunks of meat into smaller pieces so the stomach acid can get to it. Weird, and kinda gross, but common sense.

❷ **Scientific method.** The second type asks about the scientific method. Particularly, about a control in an experiment. The control is the variable that is held constant throughout the experiment. For example, if we were testing the effect of various soaps to kill germs, we might conduct one experiment without any soap to have a baseline to compare the other results. This one experiment with no soap is the **control**. It gives us some idea or **control** over analyzing the effectiveness of the soaps tested.

Let's use this on the question from the Pretest.

35. If the copper present in the samples has been there since before the area was Lake Alexander, what likely contributed to the presence of the copper?
   A. Corrosion of household plumbing systems only
   B. Erosion of natural copper deposits only
   C. Corrosion of household plumbing systems and erosion of natural copper deposits
   D. Greater distance from urban areas

Solution: Choice B. Many students say, "I have no idea." Or, they go with choice C since both are mentioned in the passage. But if the lake is thousands of years old, the copper can't be from household plumbing! The ACT actually does this. And they don't even mean it as a trick. They are testing if you are willing to think, and if you get intimidated. So, do you get intimidated? Shout with me now, "No way!"

Correct answer: B

ACT Mantra #35
Don't get intimidated. If the wording of a question is confusing, reread it a few times and then do the thing that seems most obvious. That's usually correct for ACT Science questions!

Don't Be Controlled Drills

Let's look at some type V questions:

A study was conducted to determine whether a salt/sand alternative proved effective on frozen road surfaces. Researchers predicted that a given amount of salt/sand mixture could be used interchangeably with ordinary road salt.

Ordinary road salt, composed primarily of NaCl, was compared with a 50% NaCl and 50% sand mixture. The salinity (salt concentration) of the road salt used in both was identical. The scientists gathered data from road crews in Dunnville, Ontario. The road crews reported the pounds of salt or salt/sand mixture needed for a 1-mile stretch of a two-lane road. The results are presented in the table.

Road surface temperature (°C)	NaCl (lb)	NaCl and sand (lb)	Application
>0	100	200	As needed
−4 to −1	200	400	As needed
−9 to −5	250	500	Every 3 h
−14 to −10	300	600	Every 2 h

❶ The main purpose of the experiment was to determine

  Ⓐ the number of applications of road salt needed for varying road surface temperatures

  Ⓑ the effectiveness of a salt/sand mixture in above-zero conditions

  Ⓒ the salinity levels of ordinary road salt and of the salt/sand mixture

  Ⓓ the number of pounds of ordinary road salt and salt/sand mixture needed

❷ The table shows that as road surface temperatures decrease, frequency of application of road salt increases. This is most likely so because at lower temperatures

  Ⓕ the road surface refreezes more quickly

  Ⓖ more salt is needed per application

  Ⓗ salt is more effective than salt/sand

  Ⓙ salinity decreases

❸ Researchers wanted to reduce the amount of salt used because it harms plants near the road and potentially contaminates nearby soil deposits and water tables. Does the study indicate that using the salt/sand mixture reduces the use of salt?

  Ⓐ Yes; the salinity of the mixture was identical to that of the ordinary road salt.

  Ⓑ Yes; the mixture contains only 50% salt.

  Ⓒ No; the temperatures varied and do not show consistent data.

  Ⓓ No; the pounds needed for the mixture were twice the pounds needed for ordinary road salt and therefore had equal amounts of salt.

Fight!

One passage per science test has no graphs at all. It is basically a reading passage that should have been in the Reading section. This graphless passage always provides views from two or more scientists or students who debate some theory, like why the ocean is blue. Then the questions always ask you to compare and contrast their opinions.

The key to this passage is to read each theory and then jot down or circle a few words that sum up that person's view. And watch for differences and similarities as you read; we know that we will be asked about these distinctions in the questions.

Let's look at distinctions on the question from the Pretest.

36. At a given depth, the copper concentrations at site 2 versus the copper concentrations at site 1 were
F. the same
G. lower
H. higher
J. sometimes higher and sometimes lower

Solution: Look at each site in Figure 2 and compare the values for the two sites at each depth. For 25 m, site 1 had about 0.5 ppm and site 2 had approximately 0.35 ppm, but for 30 m site 1 had 0.5 ppm and site 2 had almost 1 ppm. So site 1 was sometimes higher and sometimes lower. This question, because it is from the passage in the Pretest, uses graphs. But in the drills we'll see "fight" questions that are graphless.

Correct answer: J

ACT Mantra #36
For a "fight" passage, read the first scientist/student opinion and circle or jot down the main idea and then read the second scientist/student opinion and circle or jot down the main idea. Then consider for a moment the similarities and differences. That will answer the questions of the passage.

Fight! Drills

Two scientists explain why a study found that moose chose winter sites with more coniferous than deciduous trees. Conifers are trees that do not lose their leaves or needles in the winter.

Late winter bedding sites of moose (*Alces alces*) were surveyed in February and March of 1995 and were further examined in August of 1995 for the purpose of characterizing and comparing the habitat selected. The data was collected from 102 sampling points in February and 65 in March. Snow depth in February exceeded 50 cm. Snow accumulation in March did not reach this height.

Scientist 1

Coniferous cover is increasingly important in winter during accumulation of snow. Conifer trees do not lose their leaves in winter and provide some cover from snowfall. Moose seek out conifer tree areas for this shallow snow, which allows easier movement as well as greater availability of shrubs for browsing (eating).

Scientist 2

If snow accumulation influenced moose habitat, then moose would have sought conifer cover during February and moved out into the open during the reduced snowfalls of March. However, the March sites were characterized by a higher conifer component than were the February sites.

Results consistently indicated that conifer canopy became more significant as winter progressed. So, it was not the snow depth that attracted the moose to the conifers in March, but the crust conditions. While snow depth was reduced in March, the snow crust was softer and impeded moose movement.

1. Which of the following does scientist 1 suggest draws moose to areas of cover from snowfall?

   (A) Softer snow crust

   (B) Denser forests

   (C) More accessible shrubs

   (D) Deeper snow

2. According to the passage, which scientist(s), if either, would predict that moose in June would seek conifer cover?

   (F) Scientist 1

   (G) Scientist 2

   (H) Neither scientist 1 nor scientist 2

   (J) Both scientist 1 and scientist 2

3. Scientist 2 would most likely argue that

   (A) mobility in the snow is less important than depth of the snow

   (B) depth of snow is less important than mobility in the snow

   (C) conifer cover impedes moose mobility

   (D) deciduous trees provide more food for moose during winter months

4. The views of both scientists are similar because they imply that

   (F) ease of movement is an important consideration in moose habitat

   (G) moose favor conifer trees to deciduous trees

   (H) snow makeup determines ease of browsing for moose

   (J) moose prefer conifer cover more in February than in March

5. The hypothesis of scientist 2 could best be tested by

   (A) taking temperature readings in deciduous forests during the next 5 years

   (B) measuring snow depths under conifer cover throughout February and March

   (C) tagging moose and following them throughout the summer

   (D) analyzing data on crust conditions and moose habitats for the past 50 years

How to Be a Science Genius

Science makes anything **sound** painful, SpongeBob.

Sandy Cheeks, *SpongeBob SquarePants* (Nickelodeon, 1999)

You've now learned all the skills that you need for the ACT Science section. The Mantras remind you what to do when, what that girl who got a 36 does automatically. In Skill 37, let's make sure you've integrated the Mantras. Drill them until you are ready to teach them. Then do that. Once you're sure you've got 'em, check off the box next to each Mantra. Learning Mantras is like learning martial arts. Practice until they become part of you, until you follow them naturally: when you see a Science question, you know which type it is, you confidently find the appropriate graph, and you find the answer. Your ACT score and probably even your science class grades will go way up.

☐ **Skill 30.** Read ACT passages quickly, just to get the gist of what the experiment is generally about. Then glance at the graphs and go to the questions.

☐ **Skill 31.** The most common ACT Science question asks you to find a value or a fact from the tables or graphs. And usually the question tells you exactly which table or graph to look back at!

☐ **Skill 32.** The second most common type of ACT Science question asks you to look at a chart or graph and decide what happens to one thing as another changes.

☐ **Skill 33.** The third type of ACT Science question asks you to use the graph or table to determine the value for a data point that is not shown but is above, below, or between points that are shown.

☐ **Skill 34.** When you see a question that refers to a graph and you don't see the terms from the question in the graph, look at the paragraphs.

☐ **Skill 35.** Don't get intimidated. If the wording of a question is confusing, reread it a few times and then do the thing that seems most obvious. That's usually correct for ACT Science questions!

☐ **Skill 36.** For a "fight" passage, read the first scientist/student opinion and circle or jot down the main idea and then read the second scientist/student opinion and circle or jot down the main idea. Then consider for a moment the similarities and differences. That will answer the questions of the passage.

☐ **Skill 37.** If a question does not tell you which table or graph to use, scan the figures for the one that has the terms from the question.

Let's try this on the question from the Pretest.

37. According to Figure 1, which of the following graphs best represents the *elevations*, in meters above sea level, of the top of the sand and gravel layer at sites 1 and 2?

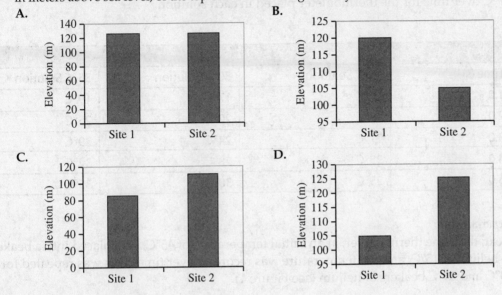

Solution: According to Figure 1, the surface of site 1 is approximately 105 m above sea level, and the surface of site 2 is approximately 125 m above sea level. Don't get scared by having to estimate 105 and 125 from the figure. Even if you said 100 and 140, you'd still get the answer. They purposely made the choices far enough apart that any decent estimate will work.

Correct answer: D

Experiment 1

A mercury thermometer, at an initial temperature of 15°C, was placed in a 25°C solution, and the temperature shown on the thermometer was recorded over time. This procedure was repeated using solutions at 30°C and 35°C. Table 1 shows the recorded temperatures in °C over time for the thermometer placed in each solution.

Table 1			
Time (s)	25°C Solution	30°C Solution	35°C Solution
1.0	16°C	17°C	19°C
2.0	18°C	20°C	25°C
3.0	21°C	24°C	29°C
4.0	25°C	28°C	32°C
5.0	25°C	30°C	35°C

Experiment 2

Next, the same thermometer, at an initial temperature of 45°C, was placed into a beaker of helium at 15°C, and the temperature was recorded over time. This was repeated for 30°C and 45°C beakers of helium (see Figure 1).

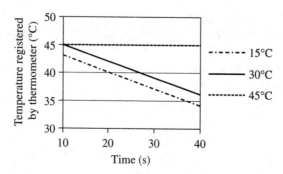

Figure 1

Choose the best answer for each question. Watch for the six types of ACT Science questions.

1 Based on Figure 1, at 25 s, the thermometer reading in the 30°C helium most likely was closest to which of the following?

Ⓐ 38.0°C

Ⓑ 40.5°C

Ⓒ 45.0°C

Ⓓ 50.5°C

2 When the thermometer was in the 25°C solution, in the time interval between 3 s and 4 s, approximately how rapidly, in °C/s, was the temperature registered by the thermometer changing?

Ⓕ 1°C/s

Ⓖ 3°C/s

Ⓗ 4°C/s

Ⓙ 25°C/s

3 According to Table 1, for a solution temperature of 35°C, over which of the following time intervals was the thermometer reading changing most rapidly?

Ⓐ 0 to 1 s

Ⓑ 1 to 2 s

Ⓒ 2 to 3 s

Ⓓ 3 to 4 s

4 Based on Figure 1, for the thermometer placed in 30°C helium, the mercury atoms in the thermometer were moving most slowly at which of the following times?

Ⓕ 0 s

Ⓖ 20 s

Ⓗ 30 s

Ⓙ 40 s

5 Based on Figure 1, if the thermometer, at an initial temperature of 45°C, had been placed in a helium sample at 5°C, how long would it most likely have taken the thermometer reading to reach 40°C?

Ⓐ Less than 20 s

Ⓑ Between 20 s and 25 s

Ⓒ Between 25 s and 30 s

Ⓓ Greater than 30 s

6 In Experiment 2, placing the thermometer into which of the following beakers of helium was used to test if the helium temperature was held constant?

Ⓕ The 15°C beaker of helium

Ⓖ The 30°C beaker of helium

Ⓗ The 45°C beaker of helium

Ⓙ The 25°C solution

7 The kinetic energy of mercury decreases as temperature decreases. Based on this information, over all samples in Table 1, as time passes, the kinetic energy of the mercury

Ⓐ increases only

Ⓑ decreases only

Ⓒ increases, then decreases

Ⓓ decreases, then increases

Essay

Like the English section, the Essay is not testing to see if you are the next William Shakespeare. It tests whether you can write an organized essay with intro, body, and conclusion paragraphs. The ACT Essay seems a mystery to many kids. But it turns out that graders are trained to look for very specific things. If you give graders what they look for, you ace the essay. In the next 11 Skills, I'll show you exactly what they look for.

Brainstorm

Okay, you're at the test center. The room smells like high school french fries and feet. The proctor has finished reading the Essay directions and tells you to open to the prompt. What do you do?

❶ Open your booklet.
❷ Read the essay topic.

Then what? Decide if you agree or disagree. Okay, not bad. Even better, start by thinking of **specific** examples that demonstrate or disprove the question. The question has no right answer, so brainstorm examples, and then take the side supported by your strongest examples.

Brainstorming **specific** examples avoids the biggest problem that kids face on the essay—using generalizations and too few details to support their point. Going straight to brainstorming **specific** details prevents you from an essay of generalizations. So brainstorm for details—names, places, dates, people, etc.

Using details is good advice for proving any point or winning any argument. Let's say you want to convince your parents to let you go to Ed's party. What works better? "Commme onnnnn, Mommmm!" or "Ed's parents will be home. His dad is head of the county chapter of Parents Against Drunk Driving, and his mom is an emergency room doctor. They plan to supervise the whole time." Details are always more powerful.

So, let's look at the question from the Pretest.

In your opinion, should high school students be required to demonstrate a passing grade average in order to take their driving test?

Solution: Okay, let's brainstorm. There is of course no right answer here. There's no right position to take or even no right or wrong examples to use. You just need to support your position, whatever it is. The key is to brainstorm for **specifics**, not generalizations. Make that small change right here, in this step of the process, and your score will go up.

Hallie, a student of mine who faced this essay question, jotted down a few specifics. She thought of kids in her school with great grades who were irresponsible drivers and kids with poor grades who were great drivers. She thought of a friend who had all A's and B's but had a car accident while searching for a CD on the floor of her car. Perfect **specific** example. We'll look at her essay in the Skills to come.

ACT Mantra #38
Brainstorm for *specific* details, not generalizations.

Brainstorm Drills

Read each of the following essay topics and then brainstorm for specific examples that prove or disprove the assignment. Based on the examples that you come up with, choose a position.

1

Many high schools have raised revenue by allowing corporations, such as Coca-Cola, to advertise on school grounds. Some school administrators believe that there is no harm in advertisements on campus since students are already exposed to the advertisements outside of school. Others believe that schools should ban advertisements on campus because students learn best in a neutral, ad-free environment, without corporations trying to sway their opinions. In your opinion, should high schools allow paid corporate advertisements on school grounds?

In your essay, take a position on this question. You may write about either one of the points of view given, or you may present a different point of view on this question. Use specific reasons and examples to support your position.

2

Some high schools have considered extending the school day to 5 p.m. so working parents can come home to supervise their children. These schools believe that students will be safer when supervised on campus than when allowed to leave at 2 p.m. Other schools believe that the school day is already too long and that students can handle the responsibility of managing their time until working parents get home. In your opinion, should high schools extend the school day to 5 p.m.?

In your essay, take a position on this question. You may write about either one of the points of view given, or you may present a different point of view on this question. Use specific reasons and examples to support your position.

Brain Freeze Help

Many kids fear brainstorming. "I might freeze!" they lament. We can absolutely prevent this. Guaranteed. The essay question **always** gives you three general viewpoints on the topic. All you have to do is take each viewpoint and make it specific. Just put a name to the general statement. You can even make one up by saying, "Imagine a person who. . . ."

Let's see this on the Pretest topic.

In your opinion, should high school students be required to demonstrate a passing grade average in order to take their driving test?

Solution: As always, the prompt provides several sides to the topic: "Failing grades indicate irresponsibility and likely an irresponsible driver. Grades and responsible driving are not related." If you were given nothing to go on, perhaps sometimes you'd draw a blank. But they give examples to use, and you can just make them specific. Plus, once you do that, more ideas will always come to you.

Let's try it:

Hallie chose to write that passing grades should **not** be a requirement, so let's look at it that way:

❶ "Failing grades indicate irresponsibility and likely an irresponsible driver."

Think of a person who has failing grades but is a good driver. Picture him or her. That person will be the focus of a paragraph. In the paragraph you will be as specific as possible.

❷ "Grades and responsible driving are not related."

Think of a person who has great grades but is a terrible driver. Picture her or him. That person will be the focus of a paragraph. In the paragraph you will be as specific as possible.

After you practice this in the Drills and Posttests, you will trust your ability to make the general viewpoints into specific examples. Of course, if something else brilliant occurs to you, use that, but if not, just use our trick. Ironically, because you come with a plan, you are more likely to be relaxed and more likely to come up with brilliant new examples that are perfect for the essay topic.

> **ACT Mantra #39**
> **When you brainstorm for details, if something new that perfectly fits the assignment occurs to you, of course use it. If not, just turn the general viewpoints from the question into specific examples.**

Brain Freeze Help Drills

Practice turning each of the two general viewpoints given in the prompts into specific examples.

❶ Many high schools have raised revenue by allowing corporations, such as Coca-Cola, to advertise on school grounds. Some school administrators believe that there is no harm in advertisements on campus since students are already exposed to the advertisements outside of school. Others believe that schools should ban advertisements on campus because students learn best in a neutral, ad-free environment, without corporations trying to sway their opinions. In your opinion, should high schools allow paid corporate advertisements on school grounds?

In your essay, take a position on this question. You may write about either one of the points of view given, or you may present a different point of view on this question. Use specific reasons and examples to support your position.

❷ Some high schools have considered extending the school day to 5 p.m. so working parents can come home to supervise their children. These schools believe that students will be safer when supervised on campus than when allowed to leave at 2 p.m. Other schools believe that the school day is already too long and that students can handle the responsibility of managing their time until working parents get home. In your opinion, should high schools extend the school day to 5 p.m.?

In your essay, take a position on this question. You may write about either one of the points of view given, or you may present a different point of view on this question. Use specific reasons and examples to support your position.

Outline

Okay, you've read the assignment, you've brainstormed for specific details, and you've started to ignore the french fry and feet smell in the cafeteria as well as the guy next to you chomping his gum. (This is why, when you do practice tests, you should hire a few people to tap pencils, chomp gum, and talk to themselves. Then you'd be truly prepared.)

So, now what? Do you make a long extensive outline? That would be nice, but really there's not time. Your brainstorm is your outline. All you need to do is circle a word or two for each example that you'll use, something that will remind you of the specifics. **Each specific example will be the focus of a paragraph.** This is very important; otherwise the essay can seem like a disorganized rant. So, to prevent this, focus each paragraph around one specific example.

For this outline, there's no time or need to jot down all the details. You know them, they are safely in your head, and you'll remember them when you need to. And if you can't recall one detail, don't worry. The graders don't know what's in your head. They have no expectations, so don't be attached to any specific piece of information.

Let's outline from our brainstorm for the Pretest.

In your opinion, should high school students be required to demonstrate a passing grade average in order to take their driving test?

Solution: Jot down or circle the best details from your brainstorm. The best details are the ones that most powerfully demonstrate your position. These examples form the outline for the body paragraphs of the essay. Each is the main idea of a paragraph.

Let's look at an example:

Specific detail: ⟨Lacrosse players at my school.⟩

The body paragraph might look something like this:

Lacrosse is very serious at my school. Varsity lacrosse players exhibit tremendous responsibility. They must be very devoted to the team and spend hours each day training. They have to show up to every practice and every game on time. They must play through discomfort, exhaustion, and even pain. Yet not every athlete has good grades. Clearly these athletes demonstrate the responsibility to be careful drivers. Perhaps a varsity letter should be required to take the driving test!

ACT Mantra #40
Jot down or circle the best details from your brainstorm. Each detail will be the main idea of a body paragraph of the essay.

Outline Drills

Circle or jot down the best details as your outline. Each detail is the main idea of a body paragraph.

❶

Many high schools have raised revenue by allowing corporations, such as Coca-Cola, to advertise on school grounds. Some school administrators believe that there is no harm in advertisements on campus since students are already exposed to the advertisements outside of school. Others believe that schools should ban advertisements on campus because students learn best in a neutral, ad-free environment, without corporations trying to sway their opinions. In your opinion, should high schools allow paid corporate advertisements on school grounds?

In your essay, take a position on this question. You may write about either one of the points of view given, or you may present a different point of view on this question. Use specific reasons and examples to support your position.

❷

Some high schools have considered extending the school day to 5 p.m. so working parents can come home to supervise their children. These schools believe that students will be safer when supervised on campus than when allowed to leave at 2 p.m. Other schools believe that the school day is already too long and that students can handle the responsibility of managing their time until working parents get home. In your opinion, should high schools extend the school day to 5 p.m.?

In your essay, take a position on this question. You may write about either one of the points of view given, or you may present a different point of view on this question. Use specific reasons and examples to support your position.

Write Your Intro

Your introductory paragraph should be short, maybe two, three, or four sentences. Make the first sentence interesting if you can—a question, a quote, a surprising statement, something clever. If you can't, that's okay, just ask or answer the question from the assignment. Then use a sentence to link that exciting statement or provocative question to your thesis that basically leads us to your opinion. Then end the intro with your thesis. The thesis clearly states your opinion and, ideally, cites the specific examples that will be the focus of the body paragraphs. Use this "opener, link, and thesis" as the format, and within that format be you—let your own style come through.

Let's apply this to the Pretest question.

In your opinion, should high school students be required to demonstrate a passing grade average in order to take their driving test?

Solution. Did the intro that you wrote accomplish opening, link, and thesis? Here's what Hallie wrote:

> There is no relationship between grades and driving skills and therefore a grade requirement in order for a student to obtain a driver's license is inappropriate and unnecessary. The ability to drive well, although connected with responsibility, is in no way connected to a student's grades.

She went right to it—two sentences, down to business. She did not start with a question, quote, or provocative statement, and that's 100% fine. It's better to have a short intro that gets the job done than one that rambles or has too much body paragraph material in it. Use an opener if something clever comes to you; otherwise, get down to business like Hallie did.

Notice that Hallie states her stance clearly. This is very important. Graders want to see a strong stance, so make sure your intro clearly states your opinion.

ACT Mantra #41
Your intro paragraph should be two to four sentences: an opener, a link, and a thesis.

Write Your Intro Drills

Now that you have your details and your outline planned, write your intro paragraph for each of the essay topics. Use opener, link, and thesis as the format, and within that be you, let your own style come through. *Note:* To provide space for your writing, I have not copied the full prompts; refer to Skill 40 Drills if you need to reread them.

1. Assignment: Should high schools allow paid corporate advertisements on school grounds?

_____

_____

_____

_____

_____

_____

_____

_____

_____

_____

_____

2. Assignment: Should high schools extend the school day to 5 p.m.?

_____

_____

_____

_____

_____

_____

_____

_____

_____

_____

Skill 42

Transition Sentences

Each paragraph should begin and end with a transition sentence of some kind. I'm not telling you to be totally boring and predictable. Just make sure each paragraph is introduced and tied up in some way.

Each paragraph should focus on one specific example. When paragraphs flow organically from one to the next, transitions happen easily. In fact, if a transition statement is very tough to come up with, perhaps the paragraphs and the thesis are too scattered. Don't worry, we will practice this so that your paragraphs flow smoothly and are not scattered.

Make your transition statements your own, and make them brilliant. If you are not feeling brilliant and creative, you can just mention the previous paragraph and/or introduce the main idea of the next, such as "Now that you know that transition sentences are important, let's take a look at one that Hallie used."

> Once again here's the question from the Pretest.
>
> In your opinion, should high school students be required to demonstrate a passing grade average in order to take their driving test?

Solution: Look at the transition sentences that you wrote. Do they introduce the main idea of the paragraph, link to the previous paragraph, and/or remind us of your thesis? Each one need not necessarily fulfill all three of these goals but should nail at least one or two of them.

Let's look at one of Hallie's transition sentences. You've seen her intro. Then she began her first paragraph with "Grades, in themselves, can be interpreted in numerous ways." This transitions nicely from the intro to the first paragraph, which is about whether grades and responsibility correlate. Each of her transition sentences links the final sentence of the previous paragraph to the main idea of the next. To see Hallie's transition sentences in context, refer to her complete essay on page 133.

If transitions are difficult for you, just introduce the main idea of each paragraph, such as

- "Another reason that grades do not predict responsible driving is . . ."
- "From a personal perspective . . ."
- "From a financial perspective . . ."

ACT Mantra #42
Use transition sentences to begin each paragraph, to link it to the previous paragraph, and/or to remind the reader of your thesis.

Transition Sentences Drills

Okay, look back at the intro that you wrote in the drills of Skill 41. The next paragraph is the first "body" paragraph, which uses a specific example that you brainstormed to demonstrate your thesis. Your transition sentence should introduce the main idea of the paragraph, link to the previous paragraph, and/or remind us of your thesis. Now let's see it:

1. Assignment: Should high schools allow paid corporate advertisements on school grounds?

_____

_____

_____

_____

_____

_____

_____

_____

_____

_____

_____

_____

2. Assignment: Should high schools extend the school day to 5 p.m.?

_____

_____

_____

_____

_____

_____

_____

_____

_____

_____

_____

A Strong Body

Keep each "body" paragraph focused around a single main idea. It's easiest to write it around one important example, with lots of details about the example. That avoids the two biggest problems that I see in students' essays: lack of details and lack of focus. Organizing around one example automatically corrects both of these! And organization is the most important factor that graders look for!

Let's look at what you did with your body paragraphs:

In your opinion, should high school students be required to demonstrate a passing grade average in order to take their driver's license test?

Solution: Make sure your body paragraphs are very detailed; the more details, the better. Usually, open with a transition sentence. You can remind us how this example demonstrates your thesis. Here's what Hallie wrote for her first body paragraph:

Grades, in themselves, can be interpreted in numerous ways. Some students who get great grades are actually very smart and some just work very hard. The difference between an A and a B doesn't necessarily have to be correlated with the person's given intelligence. This is exhibited in many schools and even films with the hero being a very smart kid who doesn't know how to apply him or herself.

Notice that Hallie's paragraph has a specific point—that good or poor grades can mean different things. She begins with a nice transition sentence. She uses generalization but follows up with specifics. She could have been even more specific, such as mentioning the film that she's thinking of, but the paragraph is strong and demonstrates her point that good or bad grades do not always mean the same thing.

ACT Mantra #43
Begin each "body" paragraph with a link to the previous paragraph, and write each around a single main idea.

A Strong Body Drills

You've already written the transition sentence. Now, let's see that first body paragraph for each of the topics:

1. Assignment: Should high schools allow paid corporate advertisements on school grounds?

_____
_____
_____
_____
_____
_____
_____
_____
_____
_____
_____
_____
_____

2. Assignment: Should high schools extend the school day to 5 p.m.?

_____
_____
_____
_____
_____
_____
_____
_____
_____
_____
_____
_____

More Body

You should have several more body paragraphs. Each one begins with a link to the previous paragraph and focuses on a single main idea, usually a single important specific example. Use as much detail as you can. Keeping each paragraph focused on one example guarantees a higher score. Organization is what graders most want to see. Focused, detailed paragraphs with transition sentences make an essay very clear and organized. Remember, this avoids the two biggest problems that I see in students' essays: lack of details and lack of focus.

> Let's look at what you did with your body paragraphs:
>
> In your opinion, should high school students be required to demonstrate a passing grade average in order to take their driver's license test?

Solution: Make sure your body paragraphs are very detailed; the more details, the better. Usually, open with a transition sentence. You can link to the previous paragraph and/or remind us how this example demonstrates your thesis.

Here's what Hallie wrote for her next two body paragraphs:

> A person's grades also do not necessarily correlate to their talent in other respects of life. Someone could be a fantastic athlete, which requires responsibility to attend practices, or an amazing actor, which requires responsibility to attend rehearsals, but not be an exceptional student. Each of these individuals might get mediocre grades but be a terrific driver.
>
> The fact is one does not need to be smart to know how to drive. Some incredibly good students are awful drivers; many top-grade teenagers have gotten into accidents as they searched the floor of their car for just the right CD. Comparing the ability to drive responsibly with the grades a person gets is similar to comparing someone's ability to play shortstop with the grades they get.

Notice that each of Hallie's paragraphs has a specific point with strong details such as "actor . . . rehersal," "searched the floor of the car . . . ," and "ability to play shortstop. . . ." Graders love these specifics. They are interesting and demonstrate Hallie's point.

ACT Mantra #44
The third or fourth body paragraph should finish demonstrating your thesis.
It should be organized around a specific example of your thesis. Ideally, it
smoothly links to your previous body paragraph.

More Body Drills

Let's see the next one or two body paragraphs for each of our topics:

1. Assignment: Should high schools allow paid corporate advertisements on school grounds?

_____

_____

_____

_____

_____

_____

_____

_____

_____

_____

_____

2. Assignment: Should high schools extend the school day to 5 p.m.?

_____

_____

_____

_____

_____

_____

_____

_____

_____

_____

_____

Body III

So far, you used specific examples to demonstrate your stance. ACT readers obviously give points for examples that prove your point. The next body paragraph should do the opposite. Readers are trained to give points for a paragraph that **disproves** the **opposite side**. This is another great debate technique; prove your point of course, but also disprove the opposition. This is also a great place to make sure you have evaluated all three perspectives provided in the essay prompt. This will earn you another point, guaranteed!

Let's apply this to the Pretest prompt.

In your opinion, should high school students be required to demonstrate a passing grade average in order to take their driver's license test?

Solution: Like all body paragraphs, this paragraph should revolve about one main idea, contain specific details, and demonstrate your thesis. Let's look at Hallie's:

> The idea of requiring a passing average to take a drivers exam is probably well intentioned. Legislators want to protect teenagers and prevent accidents. They want teenagers to prove that they are responsible enough to drive. However, while good grades are associated with responsibility, they do not guarantee it, and poor grades in no way confirm the absence of responsibility. Learning to be a good driver involves focus and also physical coordination. A person need not know all the capitals of Africa in order to look both ways and make a good right turn on red. In order to be a good driver, one must be aware and not get distracted.

Hallie mentions the other side of the argument and then disproves it. She uses details instead of generalization. Details like "capitals of Africa" and "right turn on red" make the reader more involved in the essay and make it more interesting to read. Details **always** prove a point more powerfully than generalizations do.

If this paragraph does not come easily to you, you can follow Hallie's format. Begin by paraphrasing the other viewpoint from the prompt. Then write, "However, . . ." and state a specific example that demonstrates the opposite of that view point.

ACT Mantra #45
In the last body paragraph, paraphrase and disprove the opposite stance of the argument.

Body III Drills

Let's see the next body paragraph(s) for each of our topics. Paraphrase and disprove the opposite stance on the issue:

1. Assignment: Should high schools allow paid corporate advertisements on school grounds?

_____

_____

_____

_____

_____

_____

_____

_____

_____

_____

_____

_____

_____

_____

2. Assignment: Should high schools extend the school day to 5 p.m.?

_____

_____

_____

_____

_____

_____

_____

_____

_____

_____

_____

_____

_____

Conclusion

Your conclusion should wrap it up. Generally it should follow the format: restate thesis, link, and end with a bang. The bang is like the opener. It can be a question, a quote, a surprising statement, something deep and philosophical, or something else clever. The conclusion is your last chance to prove your thesis. If you have noticed that your essay is a hair off the topic or that you have not clearly proved your thesis, you can correct this with a sentence or two connecting your examples to the assignment.

Also—and this is so important—watch your pacing and leave time for the conclusion. You'd think that they would say, "Well, s/he only had 40 minutes so I can see why s/he didn't get to it." But, no, you lose points for leaving it out. Remember, the basic thing they are testing is organization. Without a conclusion, they assume you didn't know that you needed it. So when there is, maybe, 5 minutes left, close up the body paragraph and write the conclusion. Brilliant is good, but even a modest sentence or two of a conclusion will get you points.

Let's see what you did with your conclusion.

In your opinion, should high school students be required to demonstrate a passing grade average in order to take their driver's license test?

Solution: The conclusion that you wrote should wrap up the essay. You can use "restate thesis, link, and bang." Make sure you have proved your point.

Let's look at Hallie's:

> In order to receive a driver's license, a teenager should pass their driving exam. Any other requirement is uncorrelated and futile and will not give insight into the student's abilities. Getting an A in chemistry does not assure the same grade on a driving test, just as an A on a driving test does not mean the person is a good student.

Nice conclusion. The first two sentences are a strong, crisp restatement of her thesis. Her final sentence essentially restates it again but in a clever, almost philosophical, way. Not a huge bang, but enough.

Notice that Hallie's essay is awesome but not perfect. No doubt with a few more hours she could clean it up. No one can make a perfect essay in 40 minutes. Graders know that and allow for it. They call this allowance "holistic grading." They don't have a checklist, grade each item, and add up your points. Instead, they look at the essay as a whole and say, "Okay, she had good solid organization, a few spelling errors, but wow, she blew me away with details and depth. I'll give it a 12." If you give them what they want (organization, transitions, details, depth, disprove the opposition), you get a high score. This makes the Essay easy to ace.

ACT Mantra #46
Structure your conclusion by restating your thesis, linking, and ending with a bang.

Conclusion Drills

Write a conclusion for each of our topics. Try using "restate, link, and bang."

1. Assignment: Should high schools allow paid corporate advertisements on school grounds?

_____

_____

_____

_____

_____

_____

_____

_____

_____

2. Assignment: Should high schools extend the school day to 5 p.m.?

_____

_____

_____

_____

_____

_____

_____

_____

_____

Other Stuff That Matters

You've got the format—the intro, body, conclusion essay that uses tons of specific details, analyzes the three perspectives, avoiding too many generalizations, disproves the opposition, and has nice transition sentences. What else do you need? Here are five more things that the ACT loves. Add them, and you'll gain points!

❶ **Depth of analysis.** Don't be afraid to be deep—within the safe framework of intro, body, conclusion, and with paragraphs focused on specific examples, analyze things, make insights, state your observations, make conclusions, go out on a limb. Rather than just argue the two sides, you can even give your own plan to solve the issue. Anytime I've seen a student do this, she or he gets a perfect 12!

❷ **Length.** Longer is better; it makes you look eager and smart. All else equal, longer essays score higher than shorter ones.

❸ **Big words.** The ACT loves big vocab words, so use a bunch. (But make sure to use them correctly.) If this does not come easily to you, plan a few words that you will always use. We'll practice this in the drills. This is a great way to review and learn vocab words, and it's guaranteed points!

❹ **Varied sentences.** Don't use all short, choppy sentences, and don't use all long, complex sentences. Use a variety. It makes an essay easier and more interesting to read. Variety keeps a reader awake and interested.

❺ **Readable handwriting.** Technically they don't grade for handwriting, but of course they do need to be able to read it. Try not to annoy them with handwriting that looks like the footprints left by a dying chicken. Do the best you can. Put a little extra effort into neatness. But don't stress, I have seen some pretty bad handwriting get perfect scores! Bottom line: make it readable.

❻ **Few or no grammar and spelling errors.** Make sure to proofread. Leave 2 or 3 minutes for proofing. More about this in Skill 48.

Back to the Pretest.

In your opinion, should high school students be required to demonstrate a passing grade average in order to take their driver's license test?

Solution: In your essay, did you get deep, write at least two pages, use some impressive vocab, vary your sentences, write readably, and avoid basic grammar and spelling errors?

You'll have a chance to practice these in the Drills and in the next few Skills. Adding any one of these will earn you points.

ACT Mantra #47
In your essay, get deep, write at least two pages, use some impressive vocab, vary your sentences, write readably, and avoid basic grammar and spelling errors.

Other Stuff That Matters Drills

How do you use more impressive vocab in your essay? I learned this strategy from a student who would plan several big words that he knew he would use. He got a perfect 12 every time. Obviously some words will be easier to use than others. "Ululation" (a howl) might be hard to work in, but "inherently" (naturally occurring) or "incontrovertible" (unquestionable) could be used in **any** essay. For example, "These examples demonstrate incontrovertibly that good grades do not imply responsible driving." Try this. Below are a bunch of great essay words. Use these or choose a few of your own, and try to incorporate them in the drill below. Then use them again in the practice essay in Skill 49. This is also, of course, a terrific way to review vocab words.

❶ Define each of the following great essay words:

a. Immutable_____

b. Eradicated_____

c. Auspicious_____

d. Superfluous_____

e. Affinity_____

f. Concordant_____

g. Pertinent_____

h. Thwart_____

i. Ramification_____

❷ Let's practice incorporating these tips. In the space below, take one of the body paragraphs that you wrote for Skill 44 or 45 and rewrite it, incorporating more of the following: depth of insight, length, impressive vocab, sentence variety, neatness, and proofreading.

_____

_____

_____

_____

_____

_____

_____

_____

_____

_____

_____

_____

_____

_____

_____

_____

_____

Proofread

"Write the first draft as a free write," Mrs. Schwartzonagel always said. "Don't worry about spelling and grammar, just get your ideas on paper." This was great advice, and I still use it. But for the ACT essay, it creates a mess. On the ACT, you have only 40 minutes, so attend to spelling and grammar as you write. Write quickly enough to capture your creative ideas as they come to you and quickly enough to finish in 40 minutes, but slowly enough to catch careless errors.

This is another one of those cool life skills. It's great to have the freedom and flexibility to meet different demands with appropriate measures. Like, when Big Sally gets up to bat and you say, "Back it up in the outfield!" For a long-term project, do a creative free-write. But when you are writing a 40-minute timed essay, attend to spelling and grammar as you go.

Then, when you have 5 minutes left, make sure you've done your conclusion, and use a few minutes to proofread. This is not a complex reanalysis, just a basic read over to find and correct the most common careless errors. This will definitely get you points.

Here are the most common careless errors:

1. **Omitted words.** Because you are writing quickly, your hand may leave out a word that you meant to write. Example: Critics contend that the government overspends <u>on</u> superfluous items.
2. **Obvious misspellings.** Some words you may not be sure of; do the best you can. But look for words that, of course, you know how to spell, and yet writing furiously, you misspelled.
3. **Obvious punctuation errors.** Some commas you may not be sure of; do the best you can. Fix any obvious errors.
4. **Indenting.** Make sure you indented clearly.
5. **Paragraphs.** Make sure you started new paragraphs when you meant to.
6. **Details.** Make sure you wrote what you meant to and not accidentally something else.

Back to the Pretest.

In your opinion, should high school students be required to demonstrate a passing grade average in order to take their driver's license test?

Solution: Check over your Pretest essay or Drills essays. Practice looking for and correcting the most common careless errors listed above.

ACT Mantra #48
Leave a few minutes to proofread your essay for omitted words,
misspellings, and punctuation errors, and to make sure that you
represented details accurately and started new paragraphs where you
meant to by indenting.

Proofread Drills

In the space below, quickly write a few paragraphs describing your best friend or a funny teacher. Include details and write mindfully but quickly, just like you would for the ACT Essay.

_____

_____

_____

_____

_____

_____

_____

_____

_____

_____

_____

_____

_____

_____

_____

_____

_____

_____

_____

_____

_____

_____

Now, take a few minutes to proofread your essay for omitted words, misspellings, and punctuation errors, and to make sure that you indented, started new paragraphs when you meant to, and wrote details accurately. This is great practice, and it will definitely improve your score.

Review the Mantras for our 11 Essay Skills below. Go back and reread the Skills for any that you feel unsure of. Check the box next to each Skill when you have mastered it.

☐ **Skill 38.** Brainstorm for *specific* details, not generalizations.

☐ **Skill 39.** When you brainstorm for details, if something new that perfectly fits the assignment occurs to you, of course use it. If not, just turn the general viewpoints from the question into specific examples.

☐ **Skill 40.** Jot down or circle the best details from your brainstorm. Each detail will be the main idea of a body paragraph of the essay.

☐ **Skill 41.** Your intro paragraph should be two to four sentences: an opener, a link, and a thesis.

☐ **Skill 42.** Use transition sentences to begin each paragraph, link it to the previous paragraph, and/or remind the reader of your thesis.

☐ **Skill 43.** Begin each "body" paragraph with a link to the previous paragraph, and write each around a single main idea.

☐ **Skill 44.** The third or fourth body paragraph should finish demonstrating your thesis. It should be organized around a specific example of your thesis. Ideally, it smoothly links to your previous body paragraph.

☐ **Skill 45.** In the last body paragraph, paraphrase and disprove the opposite stance of the argument.

☐ **Skill 46.** Structure your conclusion by restating your thesis, linking, and ending with a bang.

☐ **Skill 47.** In your essay, get deep, write at least two pages, use some impressive vocab, vary your sentences, write readably, and avoid basic grammar and spelling errors.

☐ **Skill 48.** Leave a few minutes to proofread your essay for omitted words, misspellings, and punctuation errors, and to make sure that you represented details accurately and started new paragraphs when you meant to by indenting.

That's it. You are ready to write a freakishly good essay. Let's go to the drills.

How to Be a Writing Monster Drills

Take 40 minutes to write an essay on the topic assigned below.

Music

Lawmakers sometimes debate whether there should be a minimum age requirement of 16 to purchase music with violent content. This raises obvious issues. Should the government get involved in sensitive parenting-related issues such as this? What constitutes violent content? Given the accessibility of purchasing and downloading music, it is worth examining the implications of this issue.

Read and carefully consider these perspectives. Each suggests a particular way of thinking about the issue.

Perspective One	**Perspective Two**	**Perspective Three**
A minimum age requirement would protect children from inappropriate messages and allow parents to make informed purchases.	The decision to purchase music should be monitored by parents and not the government.	There are different definitions of what constitutes violent content in music and it is not the government's place to assign these definitions.

Essay Task

Write a unified, coherent essay in which you evaluate multiple perspectives on the issue. In your essay, be sure to:

- analyze and evaluate the perspectives given;
- state and develop your own perspective on the issue;
- explain the relationship between your perspective and those given.

Your perspective may be in full agreement with any of the others, in partial agreement, or wholly different. Whatever the case, support your ideas with logical reasoning and detailed, persuasive examples.

Skill 50

Brian's Friday Night Spiel: Recommendations for the Days Preceding the Test

Studies show that sleeping and eating healthfully two days before the test (or any important event) is as important as sleeping and eating healthfully the night before. So Thursday night eat a healthy dinner and go to bed early—not so early that you're lying in bed at 7:00 p.m. tense, hungry, and staring at the cracks in the ceiling, but normal early, maybe 10:00 p.m.

Friday, have a normal day, no need to cram or stress. If you have completed this book and one or more timed practice tests, you are ready. Go to school, play sports or whatever you do after school, have a healthy dinner, and do something fun and relaxing. Don't hang out with anyone who stresses you out or obsesses over the test. Read, play a game, or watch a funny movie (I recommend *Fletch*, *Wedding Crashers*, or *40-Year-Old Virgin*), and go to bed at a sensible time. If you live in a household where, in the morning, everyone roams the house screaming for a clean shirt and car keys, then gather your snack, drink, admission ticket, ID, sharpened pencils, watch, and calculator in the evening.

Eat breakfast and pack a snack because it's a long day, and you have to feed the brain. For a snack, I recommend a cheese sandwich or two Luna bars; they are high in protein and not too high in sugar—good brain food. If you need an extra-special boost, in India some people take a few drops of almond oil with breakfast on the morning of a test.

Let's see if you got that.

The night before the test you should
 F. stay up all night studying
 G. go to Jules' huge party
 H. get answers from someone who is 18 hours ahead in Australia and already took the test
 J. have a nice dinner, relax, go to bed at a reasonable hour

Solution: Relax and sleep well, you are prepared. Now, go got 'em

Correct answer: J

Test Day Checklist	
2 Protein bars	Sharpened No. 2 pencils
Beverage	Calculator
Your admission ticket	Watch (to keep track of time)
Photo ID (driver's license, school ID, or passport. See act.org for more options.)	

Brian's Friday Night Spiel Drills

Here is your last drill section. Your last assignment is to be able to stay relaxed, even under pressure. So here is a little tool that you can use anytime, even during the test.

In the 1970s Herbert Benson, a researcher at Harvard Medical School, published work on what he called the relaxation response, a physiological response where the body and mind relax. Benson reported that the relaxation response was triggered by practicing 20 minutes of a concentration exercise, basically meditation.

Apparently, Yale, always in competition with Harvard, decided to one-up them. "We need a way to trigger the relaxation response, but in less than Benson's 20 minutes!" they might have bemoaned. They researched, and they tried as hard as they could to relax; it was quite stressful. Finally, someone came up with the following goofy exercise. And it is goofy, but the thing is, it works! It totally works. Do it and you'll see.

Follow these steps:

❶ Breathing through your nose, become aware of your breath.
❷ Relax your shoulders and face.
❸ Allow your exhale to be longer than your inhale.
❹ Now, drop your shoulders and head, smile, and then bring your head back up.
❺ Repeat: drop your shoulders and head, smile, and then bring your head back up.
❻ Notice how you feel.

That's it! Anytime you feel stressed, even during the test, try this very simple exercise to trigger your "relaxation response."

Score is tied: Yale, 1. Harvard, 1.

Writing the Perfect 36 Essay

Just throw away all thoughts of imaginary things
And stand firm in that which you are.

Kabir

Want that perfect 36 essay? Here are the four steps to do it.

But first you have to promise me that you are doing this because you want to, and not out of some obsessive, sleep doesn't matter, gotta please my parents, if I don't go to Tufts I'm nothing misunderstanding. Strive to do well, yes. Also stay balanced. Sleep. Eat well. Exercise. Be true to yourself. Be brave. Be honest. Be relaxed. Breathe. And from that place, give it all that you got.

❶ Make sure you understand all 11 Essay Skills and all 15 English Skills; this is the same grammar that they are looking for on the essay. Don't just look at them and say, "Yeah, I can do that." Practice. Do the drills. For the English Skills, make sure you can answer every question correctly on every Skill. If you can't, reread the section, reread the solutions, and keep redoing the drills until they make perfect sense. Then teach them to a friend.

❷ Master Posttests I, II, and III (Posttests II and III are online at www .MH-ACT_TOP50English.com). Take each test, read the solutions, and redo any questions that you missed. When you master these questions, your grammar is up to the task!

❸ Then get a copy of *The Real ACT Prep Guide*. It contains five full practice tests. Take all timed practice essays. Use our Essay Mantras to check each essay, and ask a friend, parent, or teacher to use the checklist on page 122. Practice brainstorming. Practice pacing. Practice applying the Skills.

Let's see this all put into action on Hallie and Ian's essays. Notice again that these essays do not need to be error-free, but that they contain what graders are looking for. Also don't be intimidated by these essays. I think that if essays could get a score higher than 36, these would!

Hallie's Excellent Essay

There is no relationship between grades and driving skills and therefore a grade requirement in order for a student to obtain a driver's license is inappropriate and unnecessary. The ability to drive well, although connected with responsibility, is in no way connected to a student's grades.

Grades, in themselves, can be interpreted in numerous ways. Some students who get great grades are actually very smart and some just work very hard. The difference between an A and a B doesn't necessarily have to be correlated with the person's given intelligence. This is exhibited in many schools and even films with the hero being a very smart kid who doesn't know how to apply him or herself.

A person's grades also do not necessarily correlate to their talent in other respects of life. Someone could be a fantastic athlete, which requires responsibility to attend practices, or an amazing actor, which requires responsibility to attend rehearsals, but not be an exceptional student. Each of these individuals might get mediocre grades but be a terrific driver.

The fact is one does not need to be smart to know how to drive. Some incredibly good students are awful drivers; many top-grade teenagers have gotten into accidents as they searched the floor of their car for just the right CD. Comparing the ability to drive responsibly with the grades a person gets is similar to comparing someone's ability to play shortstop with the grades they get.

The idea of requiring a passing average to take a drivers exam is probably well intentioned. Legislators want to protect teenagers and prevent accidents. They want teenagers to prove that they are responsible enough to drive. However, while good grades are associated with responsibility, they do not guarantee it, and poor grades in no way confirm the absence of responsibility. Learning to be a good driver involves focus and also physical coordination. A person need not know all the capitals of Africa in order to look both ways and make a good right turn on red. In order to be a good driver, one must be aware and not get distracted.

In order to receive a driver's license, a teenager should pass their driving exam. Any other requirement is uncorrelated and futile and will not give insight into the student's abilities. Getting an A in chemistry does not assure the same grade on a driving test, just as an A on a driving test does not mean the person is a good student.

Hallie's essay is awesome. It has a few errors, but graders loved her vocabulary, details, depth, and organization.

Ian's Awesome Essay

I would like to preface this essay by saying that I am a teenager, and that anybody responding to this question is a teenager, by definition, since they are taking the ACT. We therefore have a certain interest in this topic, and are in no way objective. In answering the question of whether or not the school day should be extended, I believe that nearly any student would say no, thank you, I have enough school, thanks. That being said, I think that there are several ways to approach this issue.

Firstly, the argument could be made, and I would agree with it, that students, especially in high school, need to learn how to live independently and not under supervision. In so many cases there is no room for transition between kids living at home, always under their parents' watchful eyes, with curfews and rules and the rest, and college. At some point parents need to trust their children because sooner or later, they will most likely end up living in a dorm, completely out of their parents' control, and it is the kids that have never had a taste of freedom that do foolish things once they are finally free of their parents tyrannical reigns.

Secondly, I can see a brilliant solution that might benefit everyone. Start schools later. Although I don't remember the sources, I have read in more than one place that studies have been conducted to test students' productivity at different hours of the day. These tests show that students are significantly better able to perform academically later in the day. I believe that students would get a great deal more out of a school day that ran from eleven to five, as opposed to one that began at eight and finished at two.

Parents that feel that their children should be occupied between the end of classes and their return from work should consider encouraging their kids to get involved in sports, student government, or any of the countless opportunities available in high schools that are not only amusing and rewarding, but make students very attractive to colleges.

I will concede there could possibly be advantages in a longer school day. High school students in the United States are often considered behind high school students in European and Asian countries. In France, for example, a typical school day begins at eight and doesn't finish until usually five in the evening.

This method, however, would not work so well in the United States. Unlike in France, our classes in high school are largely focused on class discussion and public speaking, activities that may not take as long as test-taking. The fact that our European peers may out-perform us on test-taking doesn't surprise me, since the education systems put a much more heavy focus on test-taking. In the end, I would argue that test-taking does not necessarily constitute academic competency, and frankly isn't realistic for real-life application. When will we be asked later in life to, in under an hour, summarize the bill of rights? I suggest it might be more useful to be able to think, and talk about such topics rather than be able to rattle off the facts that surround them in a short period of time.

In conclusion, I don't think that high school students in the United States need to spend any more time in school. What's more, it isn't a school's responsibility to baby-sit high school students before their parents get home from work. If parents can't figure out a solution, that's something they should probably work on with their kids.

Use the checklist on page 122 to review what graders loved about Ian's essay.

Guessing Revisited

Let's revisit what I told you way back at the beginning of the book. It will probably make even more sense now.

The ACT is not graded like a test at school. If you got 55% of the questions right on your sophomore English final, that'd be a big fat F. On the ACT Reading section, 55% of the questions right is a 21, the average score for kids across the country. If you got 70% of the questions right, that'd be a C– in school, but a nice 25 on the ACT, the average score for admission to great schools like Goucher and University of Vermont. And 85% correct, which is a B in school, is a beautiful 30 on the ACT, and about the average for kids who got into Tufts, U.C. Berkeley, University of Michigan, and Emory.

Use the above info to determine how many questions you need to answer on the ACT. If you want half correct, or 70% correct, don't rush just to finish. In school you might need to finish tests in order to do well; here you do not. You need to get to all the questions only if you are shooting for 31+.

Remember, on the ACT you lose **no** points for wrong answers. Even if you are running out of time at question #30 out of 40, you must budget a few minutes to fill in an answer for the last 10 questions. It'd be crazy not to. Statistically, if you randomly fill in the last 10 ovals, you'll get 2 to 3 correct. That's worth about 2 points (out of 36) on your score! So keep an eye on the clock, and when there are a few minutes left, choose an answer for each remaining question. Of course, when you have completed this book, you'll probably be able to finish the test and rarely even need to guess! When you do feel stumped, take another look and ask yourself, Which Mantra can I use?

Now What?

Take the Posttest. It contains questions that review the 50 Skills. Check your answers and review the Skills for any questions that were difficult. Then take the additional Posttests found online at www.MH-ACT_TOP50English.com that came with this book. Again, check your answers and review the Skills for any questions that were difficult.

After you have completed the Posttests, go to your guidance office and pick up the free packet entitled "The ACT: Preparing for the ACT," which contains a full practice test with answers and scoring instructions. Or, you can download a free test at http://www.actstudent.org.

Take the test as a dress rehearsal; get up early on a Saturday, time it, use the answer sheets and fill in the ovals. If you have competed this book, you will find that you are very well prepared. Correct and score the test and review whatever you got wrong. Figure out which Mantras you could have used to get them right.

If you have some time, purchase *The Real ACT Prep Guide*, published by Thomson Peterson's. It contains five practice tests. Take one practice test per week as a dress rehearsal. Take it when you are relaxed and focused. We want only your best work. Less than that will earn you a lower score than you are capable of and is bad for morale. Score each test and review whatever you got wrong. Figure out which ACT Mantras you could have used to get them right.

Now, you are ready, you beautiful ACT monster. Go get 'em!

Posttest I

This posttest contains questions that correspond to the 50 Skills. Take the test, check your answers, read and reread the solutions, and review the Skill sections for any that you need more help on.

One early August day last year, I <u>have been waking</u> up to the rapid flapping of wings and the agitated high-pitched cry of my cat Hissy. She, with no results, <u>were trying</u> to catch a frightened bat. I yelped, scrambled out of my bed, grabbed little Hissy, and slammed my bedroom door shut.

I barged into Jenna and Sapphire's room, and begged <u>her</u> to get it out of my room. They got up and put towels at the bottom of my door so the sly bat could not escape into the house. <u>Therefore</u>, Jenna went outside and climbed up to my roof and opened my window a crack, unaware of where the bat was lurking.

My mother <u>and I, sat,</u> anxiously watching Jenna. We waited for a long time, and then Jenna finally decided to climb into the room to check the situation. Apparently the bat had flown out without any of us even noticing. The relief was overwhelming. We had no <u>idea, however, about</u> the shots to come.

1   (A) NO CHANGE
    (B) waking
    (C) woke
    (D) had been waked

2   (F) NO CHANGE
    (G) was
    (H) trying
    (J) was trying

3   (A) NO CHANGE
    (B) them
    (C) it
    (D) its

4   (F) NO CHANGE
    (G) Then
    (H) Still
    (J) However

5   (A) NO CHANGE
    (B) and, I sat
    (C) and I sat,
    (D) and I, sat

6   (F) NO CHANGE
    (G) idea; however, about
    (H) idea, however about
    (J) idea however about

The following day, we called the doctor's office and asked if there was anything we had to do since I had <u>woken up about</u> a bat in my room. Then, the

7
news came. I needed rabies shots so that I wouldn't be foaming at the mouth or anything like that. <u>"It's</u>

8
<u>awful</u> news," my mom agreed.

I went to the Emergency Room to get my first round of shots. I went in and lay down in a bed and waited. The <u>nurses' came</u> in and said that in that

9
one day, I would <u>have to be getting</u> four shots: two

10
shots in my butt, two shots in my arms!

The pain was agonizing. Having trouble finding my <u>vein, the nurse had to inject me</u> three times. I

11
ended up passing out right after the first shot. After waking up, I got more bad news. I would have to go get more rabies vaccines, nine total!

That month was dreadful. I would sit for hours in the Emergency Room, waiting <u>greatly</u> for my name

12
to be called. Once when I was there, the Emergency

7
- (A) NO CHANGE
- (B) woken up with
- (C) woken up in
- (D) woken up from

8
- (F) NO CHANGE
- (G) Its awful
- (H) That being awful
- (J) It being awful

9
- (A) NO CHANGE
- (B) nurse's came
- (C) nurses' coming
- (D) nurses came

10
- (F) NO CHANGE
- (G) get to be having
- (H) be having to be getting
- (J) have to get

11
- (A) NO CHANGE
- (B) vein, I was injected
- (C) injections were given to me
- (D) vein, the nurse had to be injecting me

12
- (F) NO CHANGE
- (G) deeply
- (H) anxiously
- (J) intensely

Room was so crowded that the nurse giving me the shot simply put me on a rolling computer chair in the middle of the Emergency Room. The nurse started to give me the shot, but then I passed out <u>and started rolling down the hallway in the</u>
13
<u>computer chair! They had people running after me,</u>
13
<u>trying to catch me</u>.
13

14 Every time I would go, they would say, "Hey, it's rabies girl." Even the kids in my high school picked up on it. It's not my favorite nickname, but I guess it has character.

15 When I had finished my rabies series, I felt invincible. I was a pro at getting shots and could go up to any animal I wanted without getting rabies. And, even though I haven't hugged any raccoons in the past fourteen months, today I <u>was felt</u> stronger
16
and braver than ever.

⓭ If the writer were to delete the underlined portion, the paragraph would lose

Ⓐ a tie-in to the introduction

Ⓑ a transition from one sentence to the next

Ⓒ a comical anecdote

Ⓓ nothing at all, since this sentence is out of place

⓮ Which of the following true statements would best introduce the tone and focus of this paragraph?

Ⓕ After that crazy day, I had a new nickname.

Ⓖ I was invincible after surviving the shots.

Ⓗ Boy, those shots hurt!

Ⓙ I never passed out from the shots again.

⓯ Suppose the author had intended for the final paragraph to serve as a conclusion for the essay. Would the paragraph fulfill this goal?

Ⓐ Yes, because the paragraph provides many details about the rabies shots.

Ⓑ Yes, because the paragraph wraps up the writer's rabies shots experience and describes her lesson from the experience.

Ⓒ No, because the paragraph does not wrap up the essay as a whole.

Ⓓ No, because the paragraph lacks sufficient details to back up its claim.

⓰ Ⓕ NO CHANGE

Ⓖ am felt

Ⓗ feel

Ⓙ been feeling

HUMANITIES: This passage is adapted from the article "The New British Art Culture: Come Together Right Now" by Michael Brooks.

In her important and original essay "Everyone Is Creative" (which focuses on the Blair government's approach to art and pop culture), British theorist Angela McRobbie argued that
5 the Labour government has worked to put art at the "front and center" of the new British economy while at the same time pushing artists into the insecurity of the market.

McRobbie argues that artists who are thrown
10 into a market-driven system of cultural production end up reflecting "mass culture" and do not provide an alternative view, thereby limiting an essential function of art. Artists are little more than cultural entrepreneurs in a
15 system which places their focus on marketing goods. While there is undoubtedly positive development in many respects which allows for greater creative fulfillment and career choice for those with artistic livelihoods, it does dampen
20 the ability of the artist to speak freely and act in community.

While artists are now acknowledged as integral parts of the "post industrial" marketplace, and as a result given a higher social currency
25 particularly in the corporate sector, the artist has become dependent on a system of production that can stifle their own original voices. So how can artists survive in a competitive and individualist marketplace while
30 still maintaining artistic freedom and success?

There is a burgeoning movement across this country to "reclaim the commons" and this movement is incredibly relevant to the artistic community. The commons exist outside of
35 either private or government control. They are public in the fullest sense of the word. Examples of the commons include open academic research, open environmental resources, open source computer software like
40 Linux as well as folk art and oral traditions. Artists who understand the creative commons recognize that while each individual work is new and distinct they each build of a shared creative lineage.

45 For instance, Bob Dylan is a genius who shaped American music, but his work was inspired by the American folk music tradition and biblical literature and poetry. Dylan's music does not stand separate from any of these
50 currents. So while we acknowledge Dylan's unique and vital voice in the forming of American music, we also see that he built of other sources. Stanford law professor and Creative Commons founder Lawrence Lessig
55 notes the simple understanding of this collaborative process and shared innovation is seriously jeopardized by today's system of patents and intellectual property rights.

David Bollier, one of America's foremost
60 proponents of the commons, illustrates such absurd examples of over the top intellectual property rights extremism by recounting the ASCAP's attempt to charge the Girl Scouts for singing songs around a campfire and the estate
65 of J. R. R. Tolkien threatening legal action against a professional clown who called himself Gandalf.

Promoters of the commons are not attempting to separate artists from properly claiming their
70 work, rather they are responding to these ridiculous attempts at control of common cultural artifacts. The commons creates an idea of community for artists in an era of free agents. Both through different legal and financial
75 networks, but also through a strong and collaborative community the commons can help set arts in a new and free direction. This is nothing new. Artistic cultural movers from the Impressionists to the Harlem Renaissance
80 artists have always flourished in shared community.

17. The main theme of this passage concerns

Ⓐ the controversy between artists and politicians

Ⓑ the community movement in art

Ⓒ the recent instability of art gallery sales

Ⓓ absurd examples of property rights in art

18. Which of the following best describes David Bollier's opinion about the "commons" system?

Ⓕ Disregard and apathy

Ⓖ Acknowledgment of the need for its reform

Ⓗ Respect for the institution

Ⓙ Suspicion of foul play

19. As it is used in line 19, the word "dampen" most nearly means

Ⓐ make wet

Ⓑ diminish

Ⓒ make boring

Ⓓ enhance

20. According to the passage, to "reclaim the commons" refers to

Ⓕ freeing public culture from restrictive private ownership

Ⓖ tightening intellectual property rights laws

Ⓗ promoting art through academic research

Ⓙ increasing government control of artistic property

21. It can reasonably be inferred from the first paragraph that McRobbie

Ⓐ agrees strongly with the Labour government's actions regarding art

Ⓑ believes that art has little value in a time of economic crisis

Ⓒ opposes the British "commons" system

Ⓓ disagrees with the Labour government's actions regarding art

22. According to the final paragraph, which of the following best describes the author's opinion of promoters of the commons?

Ⓕ He believes that they are attempting to unjustly profit.

Ⓖ He believes that they are trying to control common cultural artifacts.

Ⓗ He believes that they are attempting to liberate art.

Ⓙ He believes that they are attempting to copy Impressionist artistic styles.

23. The main purpose of the passage can best be described as an effort to

Ⓐ explain the appeal of public ownership of artistic heritage

Ⓑ explore the need for a market-driven system of cultural production

Ⓒ examine contributing causes to the complete loss of artistic freedom

Ⓓ describe how the British government has come to the aid of struggling artists

24. The passage opens by citing an essay to introduce a topic of concern that the rest of the passage

Ⓕ paraphrases

Ⓖ debunks

Ⓗ refutes

Ⓙ explores

25. The phrase "higher social currency," as it is used in line 24, might refer to all of the following EXCEPT

Ⓐ elevated social status

Ⓑ more artistic freedom

Ⓒ increased participation in commerce

Ⓓ added economic opportunity

26 As it is used in line 51, the word "vital" means

    Ⓕ lively

    Ⓖ vigorous

    Ⓗ brisk

    Ⓙ very important

27 Which of the following best exemplifies the commons?

    Ⓐ A mural commissioned by the government

    Ⓑ A beautiful new sculpture purchased for the entryway of a corporate headquarters

    Ⓒ Collaboration between many artists to create a free website gallery of their work

    Ⓓ A national park

28 According to the first two paragraphs, McRobbie opposes market-driven art because it

    Ⓕ loses its independent and unconventional vision

    Ⓖ is of no economic value

    Ⓗ loses touch with mainstream culture

    Ⓙ reduces marketing opportunities

29 Which of the following statements would the author most likely make with regard to Bob Dylan?

    Ⓐ He is an imposter whose work is overrated.

    Ⓑ He drew upon diverse influences to create something new.

    Ⓒ His music is truly original.

    Ⓓ He would have benefited from stricter intellectual property laws.

When two male hexagon wasps encounter each other, there is a standoff until one of them backs away. The winner is referred to as "dominant." Students conducted experiments to examine the rankings of male wasps in a group. In the experiment described below, four adult male wasps were examined and then placed together in a large glass box. Their dominance interactions were observed and recorded.

Experiment 1

A student placed four hexagon wasps, referred to as wasps A, B, C, or D, into four different examining containers. For each wasp, the student recorded wingspan, age, and number of abdominal marking. The results are shown in Table 1.

Table 1			
Wasp	Wingspan (mm)	Age (days)	Number of Abdominal Markings
A	11	4	2
B	9	1	3
C	12	2	4
D	10	3	2

Experiment 2

All wasps were removed from their individual containers and then introduced into a large glass box. The student recorded their interactions in the box. In an interaction between two wasps, a wasp was labeled dominant when the other backed away. Table 2 shows the results from the interactions in the box.

Table 2				
Wasp	A	B	C	D
A	—	A dominant	C dominant	A dominant
B	A dominant	—	C dominant	D dominant
C	C dominant	C dominant	—	C dominant
D	A dominant	D dominant	C dominant	—

Based on the results of their interactions, Table 3 ranks the wasps in order of dominance.

Table 3	
	Wasp
Most dominant	C
	A
	D
Least dominant	B

30 According to the results of Experiment 1, which of the following factors is (are) related to the number of abdominal markings on an adult male wasp?

(F) Wingspan only

(G) Age only

(H) Wingspan and age

(J) Neither wingspan nor age

31 One can conclude from the results of Experiment 2 that wasp B was dominant

(A) 0 times

(B) 1 time

(C) 2 times

(D) 3 times

32 Which of the following generalizations about the relationship between wasp age and number of abdominal markings is consistent with the experimental results?

(F) The youngest wasp will have the most markings.

(G) The oldest wasp will have the most markings.

(H) The oldest wasp will have the least number of abdominal markings.

(J) Age has no effect on number of abdominal markings.

33 A fifth wasp, whose wingspan was 13 mm, was added to the experimental box. Based on the results of Table 1 and Table 3, the wasp would likely be

(A) most dominant

(B) least dominant

(C) neither most nor least dominant

(D) There is no relationship between wingspan and dominance

34 One can conclude from the results of Experiment 2 that wasp A backed away

(F) 0 times

(G) 1 time

(H) 2 times

(J) 3 times

35 It was suggested that the number of abdominal markings predict a wasp's level of dominance. Do the results of the passage support this hypothesis?

(A) Yes, because the number of abdominal markings and dominance consistently correlate.

(B) Yes, because the most dominant male hexagon wasp had the most markings.

(C) No, because the least dominant wasp had the most markings.

(D) No, because the number of abdominal markings and dominance do not consistently correlate.

36 Experiments 1 and 2 differ primarily in that

(F) Experiment 1 measures size and age of the wasps and Experiment 2 measures flight speed of the wasps

(G) Experiment 1 records characteristics of the wasps and Experiment 2 records results of their interactions

(H) Experiment 1 tests a hypothesis and Experiment 2 retests it

(J) Experiments 1 and 2 test two related hypotheses

37 The graph below reflects the relationship between wasp age and which of the following characteristics?

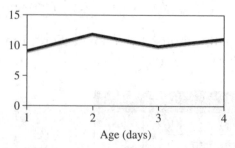

Age (days)

(A) Wingspan

(B) Number of abdominal markings

(C) Nondominance

(D) Weight

Writing Test

Time: 40 minutes

The School Day

In some high schools, students are required to enroll in a course for every period of the day. This might include academic subjects, physical education classes, art classes, and various electives. Some people think that homework should be done at home and that scheduling a class every period helps students make the most of their time at school. Other people think that schools should not require students to fill every period with a class because students need the time in a study hall to begin homework or seek extra help from teachers.

Read and carefully consider these perspectives. Each suggests a particular way of thinking about the issue.

Perspective One	Perspective Two	Perspective Three
Homework should be done at home and scheduling a class every period helps students make the most of their time at school.	Students need the time in a study hall during the school day to begin homework.	Students benefit from free periods during school to seek extra help from teachers.

Essay Task

Write a unified, coherent essay in which you evaluate multiple perspectives on the issue. In your essay, be sure to:

- analyze and evaluate the perspectives given;

- state and develop your own perspective on the issue; and

- explain the relationship between your perspective and those given.

Your perspective may be in full agreement with any of the others, in partial agreement, or wholly different. Whatever the case, support your ideas with logical reasoning and detailed, persuasive examples.

Solutions

English Skills

Skill 1 (page 19)

Subject/Verb Agreement

1. **C** Trust your ear. "Being it" sounds terrible. Try the choices. "Is it" is the only choice that sounds good. Choice B sounds very awkward, especially when you read the whole sentence. Choice D sounds weird because it's missing a verb.

2. **F** No change. The underlined verb "was" sounds fine in the sentence. It makes sense for the verb to be past tense. To be certain, try the choices. All the choices sound worse than "was."

3. **B** "I **been** in organized productions since I was . . ." sounds very slangy. Try the choices. "**I had been** in organized productions since . . ." sounds great. Choices C and D don't make sense in the context of the sentence. Your ear can hear this: "I **will have been** in organized productions **since** I was . . ." doesn't sound right because it doesn't make sense; it starts in the future and ends in the past. These drills train your ear, so you can trust it.

4. **J** "When I **were**" sounds weird because it doesn't match. It should be "when I **was**."

5. **A** No change. "What I would say" sounds great. To be certain, try the choices, and trust your ear. Choices B, C, and D sound awkward, since they are past tense, which does not fit in for the underlined words.

6. **H** "What will work . . . are" sounds weird; "are" is for a group, while "what" is usually one thing. "What will work . . . is" sounds great. Choice J, "What will work . . . has been," sounds okay at first, but not with the rest of the sentence; it's talking about something that used to happen in the past, while the sentence is talking about what works all the time.

7. **B** The two underlined verbs must match. "Be listening and react" sounds weird because the two verbs don't match. The verbs in choices B and C match, but only choice B sounds smooth in the sentence.

Skill 2 (page 21)

The One Subject/Verb Agreement Trick

1. Margarita, with her sisters, currently **runs** a marketing firm.

2. The way of all samurai **is** a strict path.

3. The boys, with their dog Alfred, **walk** to school.

4. The PTA, through generous donations, **is** building a new school building.
(Notice that "PTA" is singular and gets the singular verb "is." Organizations or groups, like "the corporation," "the 12th grade," or "My Chemical Romance" are singular. Even though the group has more than one member, the group itself is considered singular.)

1. **C** When you see a verb underlined, ask, "What is the subject?" Cross off prepositional phrases and notice what is doing the action of the verb. It looks like "cookies **have** been" is correct, but the subject of the underlined verb "have been written" is "procedure," not "cookies," so it should be "procedure . . . cookies **has** been written." Your ear can hear this anyway, but now you can prove to yourself what your ear already knew.

2. **F** No change. Your ear hears that the underlined words sound good, but here's the proof. It might seem that "butter **have softened**" should be "butter **has softened**," but "butter" is not actually the subject of the underlined verb "have softened." Cross out the prepositional phrase and "sticks" is the subject: "sticks of butter **have softened**."

3. **A** No change. When you see a verb underlined, ask yourself, What is the subject? Cross off prepositional phrases and notice what is doing the action of the verb. In this case,

what is doing the "is-ing"? Not the "sugars," but the "one-half cup." "One-half cup ~~of brown and white sugars~~ is added." I love these, they are tricky, but we expect them and get them right!

4. **G** Cookies" is the subject and "~~on the middle rack~~" and "~~of the oven~~" are prepositional phrases, so "becomes ready" should be "become ready." "**Cookies**, baking ~~on the middle rack of the oven~~, **become** ready, . . ."

Skill 3 (page 23)

Pronoun Clarity and Agreement

1. **D** When you see a pronoun underlined, identify the noun that it refers to. "**It is**" refers to the plural "cookie cutters" and should be "**they** are."

2. **F** No change. The pronoun "them" correctly refers to "options."

3. **C** This is a great example of our most important English section strategy. Make sure to read what is really written; don't correct it in your mind. The pronoun "those" refers to "cookie cutter," but "those" is plural and "cookie cutter" is singular. So "those" should be "each." It's easy to accidentally read "cookie cutter" as "cookie cutters" to make the underlined pronoun "those" work; make sure to read what's really written and not accidentally change something to make it correct!

4. **G** The pronoun "she" is unclear. Even though we are smart and know that it can only refer to "my grandma," technically in the paragraph it's not clear. Usually, a pronoun refers to the nearest important noun, which here would be "shapes." Ask yourself, What would Borat think if he translated this sentence? He would think that "she" refers to "shapes," so we must replace it with something clearer.

5. **A** No change. The pronoun "each" refers to "cookie" and matches perfectly. Choice C

is incorrect because "this" should refer to a cookie we are already talking about. And choice B is redundant (Skill 10 Preview); "each and every" is used in slang speech, but "every" is implied by "each" and is unneeded. The ACT always favors clear, concise, and not redundant.

6. **H** The pronoun "it" refers to "crystals" and should be the plural "they." When you see a pronoun underlined, identify the noun that it refers to. Choice J is wordy and should say "end," not "ends."

Skill 4 (page 25)

Correct Transition Word

1. **C** Trust your ear. "Otherwise" sounds weird and makes the sentence hard to understand. When you don't understand a sentence, don't say, "Well, I can't do this one." Say, "I don't understand that, so there must be an error!" Try the choices. Choices B and D do not clear things up, but choice C makes the sentence work. The two parts of the sentence oppose each other, so the opposition word "although" works.

2. **F** No change. The transition word "though" works because the two parts of the sentence oppose each other, and "though" is an opposition word. All of the other choices are direct cause-and-effect words, not opposition words.

3. **B** "Since" is a direct cause-and-effect transition word, but the two parts of the sentence oppose each other. So "since" is wrong, and we need an opposition word. The only one in the choices is "while."

4. **J** The transition word "whereas" actually sounds fine and seems to work, until you get to the word "however" in the same sentence. The two transitions are redundant and make the sentence very confusing. "However" is not underlined, so we cannot eliminate it, and we must delete "whereas."

5. Ⓐ No change. "For example" is a direct cause-and-effect word that fits well here, since the example in the sentence demonstrates the previous statement.

6. Ⓖ Trust your ear. The transition word "therefore" sounds very awkward because it's redundant with "in truth."

Skill 5 (page 27)

Relaxing Commas

1. Ⓓ We don't need a pause between "room" and "is." In fact, a comma should never be sandwiched between the subject and verb of a sentence.

2. Ⓗ Try this with and without a pause. Without a pause the sentence gets jumbled; it incorrectly sounds like the memories are from the three-year-old birthday poster. So which pause do we need? A comma is correct since the phrase after the pause could not stand on its own. Skill 6 Preview: If it could stand alone, then a semicolon or a comma with "and" would work.

3. Ⓓ "The rugs underfoot being always dusty" sounds awkward. We need a pause. Choice D is correct since "always dusty, always comforting," are side notes, inessential to the sentence, and therefore need commas. The "really" in choice B is slangy and unneeded, and the "are" in choice C is redundant with the "are" several words later.

4. Ⓕ No need for any pauses here. Trust your ear. You can hear it.

5. Ⓒ You can hear that we need a pause between "wall" and "blue." The phrase "blue and red" is a side note, inessential to the sentence, so we use commas. Choice D almost works, but "being" is awkward and unneeded.

6. Ⓙ Transition words, like "though," are usually surrounded by commas. Choice G is incorrect because it's the wrong transition, direct instead of opposition. Choice H is incorrect because we would only use a semicolon to separate two parts of a sentence that could each stand alone.

7. Ⓑ This sentence is missing a verb, so choice B is correct.

Skill 6 (page 29)

Are You Independent?

1. Ⓒ A comma or dash is used to separate two parts of a sentence when one of the parts could not stand alone. So choices B and D are okay, since the second part of the sentence has been changed in these choices to be dependent. A period or a semicolon is used when both parts could stand alone. Therefore, choice A works, but choice C does not, since "teaching that . . ." has no subject for the verb and could not stand alone.

2. Ⓖ We do not need a pause here. Try it with and without a pause, and your ear can hear that we don't need one.

3. Ⓓ We don't need a pause here. We would only use a period (choice A) or a semicolon (choice B) if both parts of the sentence could stand alone, but "and the world around them" cannot stand alone. It does not need a comma because it's not a side note; it goes with "understand themselves."

4. Ⓕ No change. The comma is correct, since the second part of the sentence "beginning at birth . . ." could not stand alone.

5. Ⓐ No change. Transition words, like "however," are usually surrounded by commas or a semicolon and a comma. We use commas if they separate a dependent clause, and we use a semicolon and a comma if they separate two independent clauses. "However" divides this sentence into two independent clauses, so "stages; however," is correct.

Skill 7 (page 31)

Correct Preposition

1. Ⓒ "Helping out **on** Miss Kelly's study halls" sounds strange; it should be "helping out **in** Miss Kelly's study halls." That makes sense if you think about it; he literally helped "in," not "on," the study hall.

2. **G** "**In reading**" sounds weird; it should be "**to read.**"

3. **A** No change. "**On** his . . . test" sounds great. The other choices sound awkward.

4. **J** "Never said a word **on** it to me" sounds very slangy; it should be "never said a word **about** it to me." This is great practice. You actually might use "word **on** it" or another of the answer choices in a slang way, but for formal use, only "about" works. That makes sense, since Nick literally spoke "about" it, not "on," "by," or "for" it.

5. **B** "Cared **for** the grade" sounds weird; it should be "cared **about** the grade."

6. **J** "On being" sounds weird and slangy; it should be "to be."

Skill 8 (page 33)

It's Me

1. **C** To test if "I" is correct, just drop "Manuel." Then it reads "Sometime in college, **me** had heard," which sounds terrible, so it should be "Sometime in college, **I** had heard." Choice B does not need the comma (a comma is never sandwiched directly between a subject and verb), and choice D is wrong because it just swapped the order of the words "Manuel" and "me."

2. **H** "Its" is possessive, and "it's" means "it is." So we need "it's," and choice H is best. Choice G also corrects the "its" problem but is too wordy.

3. **A** No change. "Its" is possessive and "it's" means "it is." So we need "its," and there is no change. Also, the singular pronoun "its" correctly refers to "a yoga practice."

4. **J** To test if "I" is correct, just drop "Manuel." Then it reads "Someone brought tea to **I**," which sounds terrible, so it should be "Someone brought tea to **me**."

5. **C** To test if "he" is correct, just drop "his student." Then it reads "I was listening to a story about he," which sounds terrible; so it should be "I was listening to a story about him," which sounds better.

6. **F** No change. "Who" versus "whom" is probably harder for your ear to pick up, so just plug in "I" versus "me" instead of the "who" versus "whom" and trust your ear. "**I** can see" sounds good, and "**me** can see" sounds terrible. Since "I" corresponds to "who" and "me" corresponds to "whom," it should read "**who** can see."

Skill 9 (page 35)

A Few More Rules

1. **A** No change. "Who" is used for people, and "which" is used for things. The "band," though composed of people, is considered a thing, so "which" is correct.

2. **H** Because we are watching for it, this seems ridiculously easy. But that's the key, to know that sometimes the ACT throws in an unneeded "ly." If you watch for it, it's easy!

3. **B** "They can not only deconstruct **and** also . . ." sounds awkward. "Not only" should be followed by "**but** also."

4. **F** No change. "Their" correctly refers back to "disparate pieces." Use the process of elimination. "It's" means "it is," and the other choices sound terrible.

5. **C** "Groups" is plural, so the possessive is "groups'."

Skill 10 (page 37)

Direct, to the Point, Not Redundant

1. **D** All answers besides choice D are redundant; they say the same thing twice. The ACT likes clear and concise and not redundant.

2. **H** "Stress and tension are breathed out" is passive voice. The ACT likes active voice (no offense, Yoda). Choice H is most direct and

active. Your ear can hear it; it's the most clear and direct, and the most powerful of all the choices.

3. **B** The ACT loves to use this type of question. "And less tight" basically defines "relaxed," so "relaxed, and less tight" is redundant. Choice B is the only one that corrects this.

4. **J** The underlined portion of the sentence is very wordy and muddled. Choice J is clear, direct, and concise, and it uses active voice. Your ear can hear that it is the best choice. Also, notice that choice J is the only choice that is a direct instruction, like the rest of the passage.

5. **D** "Ready and all set" is redundant, since "all set" pretty much defines "ready." So we don't need "all set," and choice D corrects that best.

6. **J** No need to say "open your eyes and with open-eyes." It's redundant. We can omit "with open-eyes." You're probably pretty bored by now of this redundancy strategy, but that's great. Every ACT has several of these questions, and now you know to watch for them, and you'll get them right!

Skill 11 (page 39)

Misplaced Phrases

1. **D** The sentence makes it sound like "the city" had "the fresh air of its open pasture," which makes no sense. "With the fresh air of its open pasture" should be as close to "farm" as possible, since it is describing it. So choice D is best. Seems like a picky thing? It is, but at least we know to watch for it and we can catch it every time. If there were a million of these picky things, that'd be tough, but there are only a few.

2. **H** The sentence makes it seem that "of Rice Krispies" describes "Grandma," when of course it describes "breakfast." Choice H is the best revision. You might even be able to think up a better way to phrase it, but of the choices, H is best. Use the process of elimination; cross out

choices that violate a rule, and pick the best of what is left.

3. **C** The sentence makes it very unclear to what the descriptive phrase "in the fields baling hay" applies. It applies to "the workers," so it should be as close to them as possible. Remember, when you read a sentence and it does not make any sense, that's because it's wrong. So read the choices and see which one makes most sense.

4. **F** No change. The sentence sounds fine, and all of the choices are wordy or have misplaced phrases. For example, choice G makes it seem that "with its familiar smell" refers to "I" rather than "Grandpa's work shirt."

5. **B** The sentence makes it seem that "the memory" has "rhythm and simplicity" when it should be the "time I spent." Choice B is the clearest revision. Choice C sounds good at first, but "the time of the memory" does not make sense. That's a great reminder to read the whole answer choice, and not just the first few words.

Skill 12 (page 41)

Word Choice

1. **C** "Demonstrates" sounds a bit strange in the sentence. Try the choices and trust your ear. Choice C sounds perfect, "The hit TV show *Entourage* **portrays** a young movie star. . . ."

2. **G** "Contests" sounds a bit strange in the sentence. Try the choices and trust your ear. Choice G sounds perfect: "the main character, Vince, faces **competition** from other actors. . . ."

3. **C** "Known to" sounds terrible in the sentence. Try the choices and trust your ear. Choice C sounds perfect: "when he was **scheduled to** go on a late night talk show. . . ."

4. **H** "Much" sounds a bit weird in the sentence. Try the choices and trust your ear. Choice H sounds perfect, "with so **many** loyal fans." In fact, "much" is used to describe something that cannot be counted or numbered, like "this

much rain," and "many" is used to describe something that can be counted, like "this many **inches** of rain."

5. **B** "Inefficient" sounds a bit off in the sentence. Try the choices and trust your ear. Choice B sounds perfect: "Vince is not **indifferent**. . . ." "Indifferent" would mean he does not care. "Absent" would not make sense, and "caring" means the opposite of what the sentence intended.

6. **F** No change. "Long-shot" sounds fine in the sentence. Try the choices and trust your ear. None of the choices sounds better.

7. **D** "Trickle" does not sound quite right in the sentence. Try the choices and trust your ear. Choice D sounds better. He pursues the long-shot because it gives him a "huge **surge**" of excitement, not a "huge trickle" or "huge tweak" of it.

Skill 13 (page 43)

Flow

1. **A** No change. The sentence as it is ties to the conclusion, since the phrase "clothing-optional" is used in both. Choice D is also in both but does not make sense in this sentence. Skill 14 Preview: These questions often confuse students until they realize that they just have to meet the **goal** stated in the question. Several answers look like valid substitutions for the underlined words, but only one answer meets the specific **goal** stated in the question.

2. **J** Adding the sentence "the 1970s saw an oil crisis and the growth of the environmental movement" would distract from the purpose of the paragraph. The purpose is to introduce the essay topic, which is a person's experience with his or her family's "clothing-optional" beach. So more info about the 1970s is not relevant and would be distracting in the paragraph. Skill 15 Preview: For a yes/no question, choose an answer that applies to the entire question and not just a few words of it.

3. **C** Each paragraph should focus on a single main idea. "I kept away" begins a new main idea, the writer returning to his or her family's beach, while the previous paragraph was about leaving the beach.

4. **J** The underlined sentence is unnecessary to the paragraph and distracts from its flow and focus.

Skill 14 (page 45)

Goal Questions

1. **C** Choice C is the one that best meets the specific **goal** of linking the first two sentences, birth to nickname. Choice A mentions Anacostia but is not a complete sentence.

2. **G** All of the sentences are interesting and would add to the paragraph, but only choice G meets the specific **goal** to "briefly describe the content of the autobiography." These questions often confuse students until they realize that they have to meet the **goal** stated in the question. Several answers look valid, but only one answer meets the **goal**.

3. **C** Choices B, C, and D are all good conclusions. But choice C best meets the **goal** to "maintain the tone established in the introduction," since it refers to the language of the intro with "Sage of Anacostia." Choice B is second-best but has no direct reference to the introduction.

Skill 15 (page 47)

Yes or No?

1. **D** The essay does not summarize "the curriculum at the top three schools." The essay just provides a general overview. Yes/no questions are a type of goal question, and we need to meet the specific goal stated in the question. Make sure to choose an answer that applies to the entire question and not just a few words of it. Choice C is incorrect because the passage says that we know "little"—not "almost nothing"—about their training; the

third paragraph even mentions what we do know about their training, but not about "the top three schools."

2. **H** The statement "The truth is that" is redundant. The writer would not make a statement in this kind of factual essay unless it were true, so we do not need "The truth is that."

3. **C** A conclusion should wrap up an essay and bring some closure. It might restate the thesis or main idea of the essay, it might use language that reminds us of the introduction, and it might recap the main points of the essay. This paragraph does none of these and is not a conclusion.

Skill 16 (page 50)

How to Think Like a Grammar Genius

1. **C** "Well known" defines "famous," so "famous well-known" is redundant. Choice C, deleting "well-known," is the best correction.

2. **H** "Different times **of** history" sounds weird. Try each choice and trust your ear. "Different times **in** history" sounds great. The "times" are literally **in**, not **of**, history. Choice J is too slangy.

3. **D** The word "originally" and the verb "married" tell us that the sentence relates to the past, so the underlined verbs should also be past tense: "lived . . . and depended." The other choices are not past tense.

4. **G** Try this one with and without the pause. No pause sounds strange, jumbled, and rushed. We need a comma after "easier." We use a comma, not a semicolon, since the first part of the sentence is dependent.

5. **B** The "its" used here means "it is" and should be "it's." Remember that "its" is possessive, like "a bear defends its cubs."

6. **F** No change. Most people find it very hard to hear when "who" or "whom" is correct, so we make it easy, and use "I" versus "me" instead. "I" corresponds to "who" and "me" corresponds

to "whom." In this sentence, "I complete them" sounds fine, and "me complete them" sounds weird. So "I" is correct, which means "who" is correct. Notice that choice J is not correct, since "which" is used with things, and "who" or "whom" is used with people.

7. **C** The clause "the person that makes them feel at ease" is dependent—it could not stand alone. It leaves you waiting for the action. Choice C is correct. Choices A and B are incorrect because a period or semicolon is used to separate two independent clauses that could stand alone. Choice D is incorrect because, without a pause, the sentence sounds jumbled.

Reading Skills

Skill 17 (page 53)

Bold Introductions

1. The passage is **prose fiction** so it will definitely be followed by questions about characters' feelings and relationships. This bold intro actually gives us a short plot summary, "The story is set in the mid-1990s in Hoboken, New Jersey, where the narrator and her friend have moved after graduating college." And we can assume that a tuna casserole, mentioned in the title, will be significant in the story.

2. The passage is **social sciences** so it will be followed by questions about details in the passage and about the writer's beliefs. The title tells us that the passage will be about Martin Luther King Jr. as a hero.

3. The passage is **humanities** so it will be followed by questions about details in the passage and about the writer's beliefs. It appeared in a University Review so it will probably be analytical. Judging by the title, the paper will analyze Will Farrell and examine if he is a jester or a genius.

4. The passage is **natural science** so it will be about sciency stuff, but it will NOT expect you to know any science; everything will be

explained in the passage, and questions will ask about details in the passage. It will probably involve "Life on Other Planets." This bold intro also gives us some info about the narrator.

5. The passage is **social sciences** so it will be followed by questions about details in the passage and about the writer's beliefs. The title tells us that the passage will be about comic books. You might catch the "Darkest Night" reference to the popular "Dark Knight" Batman comics (and movies), which will probably be mentioned. However, of course, you will not be expected to have prior knowledge, and you should answer questions based on info in the passage, not on your own beliefs or outside knowledge. Also, the words "darkest" and "obsession" hint at a negative tone in the passage.

6. The passage is **humanities** so it will be followed by questions about details in the passage and about the writer's beliefs. The intro tells us that the passage describes a young man's search for his sister, and the title indicates that his search probably occurred after a war, when people were "rebuilding and reconnecting."

Skill 18 (page 55)

The ACT Reading Meditation

1. Main idea: The narrator left home and his new wife to travel.
   Attitude/tone: Narrator becomes engrossed in travel but begins to regret his absence from his wife.

Skill 19 (page 57)

"Facetious" Most Nearly Means

1. **C** The next line indicates that the Anglo-Saxons had moved from Scandinavia and northern Germany. So they were **settling** their new home. There is no mention in the passage

about agriculture, crops, or even warfare between clans.

2. **J** The next line tells that the men were "asleep" in the hall when Grendel attacked. So "passed the hours of darkness" means that they were sleeping. Don't be tricked by choice H; the word "safety" is used in the passage, but they did not "emerge into safety." Make sure that the whole choice, and not just one word, makes sense with evidence from the passage.

3. **B** The sentence tells that Beowulf leaped up, **unexpected**. He faked being asleep, and that's why he was unexpected. "Feigned" means "faked."

4. **G** The sentence tells that Beowulf and Grendel "had an epic battle, **tearing the great hall apart**." So the best choice is G, "massive and destructive." The other words fit well with "battle," but only choice G is supported by the evidence in the passage, "**tearing the great hall apart**."

5. **A** The following sentence states, "He rewarded Beowulf with . . . a family heirloom." So "never stingy with accolades" means that he rewards generously. There is no mention of him killing Beowulf, naming Beowulf his successor, or giving to charity.

Skill 20 (page 59)

Direct Info

1. **C** Use the process of elimination. The first two paragraphs compare the two quakes. The first paragraph states that the two earthquakes had **similar** magnitudes and **similar** slip seismic disturbances, so eliminate choices A and D. The last sentence of the paragraph states that the Kocaeli quake had a larger magnitude, so choice C is correct. And nowhere in the passage does it state that **both** quakes happened in California; it says that Loma Prieta was in California and only that Kocaeli was in the city of Izmit.

2. **F** Scan your circled key words and the passage for "precautions." The third paragraph discusses precautions. It mentions several precautions but says that the most important is to "ensure nothing is built on significant faults." It does mention preparing structures, but it continues to say that avoiding fault lines is **most** important.

3. **B** Scan your circled key words and the passage for "the epicenter of Loma Prieta." The second paragraph discusses the epicenters of the quakes and states that the epicenter of the Loma Prieta quake was "significantly outside dense population centers," as opposed to Kocaeli, which was in a city. Use the process of elimination. The paragraph does say that the quake was **close to Santa Cruz**, but not **in the middle of the city**.

4. **J** Scan your circled key words and the passage for "the North Anatolian fault." It was mentioned in the first paragraph, "Kocaeli along the North Anatolian fault." So since Kocaeli was in Izmut, the fault must be closest to Izmut. The other three choices go with the Loma Prieta quake.

5. **D** This question tells you to look in the third paragraph. "Geologic material they rest on" is followed by "or, even better, to ensure nothing is built on significant **faults** in the first place." So **the material they rest on** refers to the **possibility of a fault line**.

Skill 21 (page 61)

What Are You Trying to "Suggest"?

1. **B** The second paragraph states that Jinnah "sought **protective** space for the subcontinent's **minority** Muslim population." Use the process of elimination:

   (A) was highly Westernized—No, the paragraph states that he was interested in promoting Western secular government, not that they were highly Westernized.

   (B) was being ill-treated—Okay, if he sought **protective** space, perhaps he felt they were being ill treated.

   (C) was protective of their Indian heritage—No, this may or may not be true, but it is not mentioned in the paragraph in any way.

   (D) did not want an independent state—No, this is not mentioned at all in the paragraph.

2. **H** Several of the words in the answer choices are mentioned in the passage, but only choice H captures what Jinnah suggests. He mentioned "personal piety and **universal tolerance**" to imply that Muslims should be personally devout but **tolerant** of **others'** beliefs. This is supported by the rest of the paragraph, which states that "western style democracy" would support this tolerance and that Jinnah wanted an Islamic ethic, or set of principles, but a Western, or democratic, government.

3. **C** The "motivations of the nation's founder" refer to Jinnah's intentions discussed in the second and third paragraphs. Let's use the process of elimination.

   (A) Jinnah's desire for an Islamic government in Pakistan—No, he wanted an Islamic ethic, but a **Western** government.

   (B) Jinnah's hesitance to leave India—No, this was never mentioned.

   (C) Jinnah's plan for a secular government in Pakistan—Maybe, especially if you know that secular means "nonreligious."

   (D) Jinnah's plan for a free India—No, he worked toward a free Pakistan.

Even if you didn't know the meaning of "secular," you could get this one with the process of elimination!

Skill 22 (page 63)

Some Attitude

1. **B** Attitude is expressed in the author's choice of words and punctuation. Most of the passage expresses **frustration**: "irritated," "pounding," "clanging," "blinding," and "grueling." The tone changes from frustration to **relief**, with the line "Finally, after a **grueling** mile or two, the traffic

speed **picked up**, and I was <u>freed</u> from the city." To find the answer, use the process of elimination; the words in the line do not express fear, haste (rushing), or humor. Make sure to choose the best answer, the one in which **both** words are appropriate.

2. Ⓗ The author expressed an attitude of **reverence** through words such as "peacefully," "quiet tradition," "harmony," "prayer," and "devotion." Here's the process of elimination:

   Ⓕ ~~Pleasure lessened by fear~~—No, fear was not expressed before troops invaded.

   Ⓖ ~~Enjoyment mixed with guilt~~—No, guilt was not expressed.

   Ⓗ Reverence—Yes, "reverence" means "respect."

   Ⓙ ~~Suspicion~~—No, suspicion was not expressed.

3. Ⓑ The author showed the prison officials' disapproval of the conventional criminal justice system with the statements "this approach doesn't work," and "What can we do differently?" So they did not express **disregard and apathy** (lack of interest) or **respect**, or **suspicion of foul play**, but **acknowledgment of the need for reform**.

4. Ⓙ The passage is describing a scientific study. Use the process of elimination. It is not apologetic, hostile (antagonistic and unfriendly), or tense. The author is explaining the study, but not apologizing. And you may feel hostile or tense about the study, but that is not the author's tone. The author is just describing the study.

Skill 23 (page 65)

Main Idea

1. Ⓑ Most of the choices are mentioned in the passage, but the main idea, the primary purpose of the passage, is to demonstrate Olmsted's vision. Let's find evidence: it is demonstrated by the words "foresaw," "anticipated," and "see into the future."

2. Ⓕ Interesting, all are mentioned in the paragraph. But only choice F is the **main idea**. Here's the process of elimination:

   Ⓕ the controversy between residents of Paris and the tower's designer—Yes, the paragraph describes the residents' concerns and the designer's response.

   Ⓖ ~~the inconvenience and danger posed by the tower~~—No, that is mentioned, but it is **one** detail, and not the main idea.

   Ⓗ ~~the instability of the tower in harsh weather~~—No, that is mentioned, but it is **one** detail, not the main idea.

   Ⓙ ~~Gustave's petition against the tower~~—No, Gustave was the designer, not the petitioner.

3. Ⓒ Find the evidence: It seems the author is recollecting, but "If we had a tree like this . . ." proves that it is actually a fantasy.

Skill 24 (page 67)

Gretchen Is "Such" a Good Friend

1. Ⓑ The third and fourth paragraphs describe the characters "circling" the Opera House repeatedly and give a feeling of **repetition**. The paragraphs do not provide specific details about the Opera House, contrast the soldier to Dan, or describe the economic conditions of the area.

2. Ⓙ The author italicizes the word "even" to emphasize it and to imply that if *even* the tour agencies are closed, then *every store* must be closed.

3. Ⓒ The passage opens with the question "Would we find Dan?" And the rest of the passage answers the question with the characters' search and ultimate discovery of Dan.

4. Ⓕ The final paragraph concludes the passage and answers the question from the intro by describing how the characters found Dan. The other choices have words from the paragraph but are not the main function, which is to conclude the essay. Do not be confused by

choice J, which uses the word "conclude," but has no evidence in the passage—the paragraph does not give a new set of questions. Make sure that all of the words of a choice work, not only the first or first few.

Skill 25 (page 69)

Superbad Vocab I

1. philanthropy—love for humankind or generosity
   philosophy—love of knowledge or a system of thought
   technophile—a person who likes technology
   technophobe—a person who fears technology
   technology—the study of devices
   phobia—a fear

   "phil" means "love"
   "anthro" means "humans"
   "soph" means "knowledge"
   "tech" means "devices or tools"
   "phobe" means "fear"
   "ology" means "study of"

2. homogeneous—having the same nature
   heterogeneous—having a different nature
   homosexual—attracted to one's own sex
   heterosexual—attracted to the opposite sex

   "homo" means "same"
   "hetero" means "different"
   "gen" means "kind" or "birth"

3. circumscribe—to draw around
   circumnavigate—to sail or fly around
   circumvent—to get around something
   recirculate—to circulate again
   transcribe—to translate
   circumambulate—to walk around something

   "circum" means "around"
   "scribe" means "write"
   "re" means "again"
   "trans" means "across"

4. infrasonic—sound below human hearing
   infraorder—the category below order

"infra" means "below"
"sonic" means "relating to sound"

5. *Pirates of the Caribbean: The Curse of the Black Pearl* (Walt Disney, 2003). "Cessation" means "end" or "termination." "Hostilities" means "fighting" or "aggression." "Disinclined" means "reluctant." "Acquiesce" means "give in" or "assent, comply, concede, or yield."

6. *Monty Python and the Holy Grail* (20th Century Fox, 1975). "Exploiting" means "taking advantage of." "Imperialist" means "royal" or "imposing." "Dogma" means "system of belief," "canon," "tenets," or "creed." "Perpetuates" means "continues." "Inherent" means "natural," "in-built," or "intrinsic."

Skill 26 (page 71)

Superbad Vocab II

1. "Diverting" has Spanish word "divertir," which means "to entertain." That's perfect because in English "diverting" means "fun."

2. "Facile" sounds a lot like the Spanish for "easy." Great, because in English it means "very easy or simple."

3. "Luminance" sounds a lot like the French word "lumiere" for light. Good, because in English it's a fancy word meaning "the condition of emitting or reflecting light."

4. "Clairvoyant" sounds like the French words "clair," meaning "clear," and "voyant," meaning "seeing." Does "clairvoyant" mean "clear seeing?" Yep, pretty much, or at least enough to get a sense for the word. It means "someone who sees things beyond normal vision."

5. In French, "comportement" means "behavior," which is exactly what "comportment" means in English!

6. In French, "fille" means "daughter," which is a pretty good lead, since in English "filial" means "pertaining to a son or daughter."

7. "Arid" was actually a word on my SAT (we didn't have the ACT in New Jersey back in

1988). I didn't know it, but I remembered a TV commercial jingle for the antiperspirant deodorant Arid Extra Dry. I thought, "If Arid is the name of a deodorant, there's no way it means 'smelly' or 'foul' or 'wet' or anything bad; it must mean 'smells good' or 'dry' or 'attractive,'" and that was enough to vibe the word and get the question correct. "Arid" means "very dry."

8. The "Impervious Charm" is the one that makes things repel substances like water, and "impervious" means "impermeable" or "resistant."

9. "Stupefy" is the Stunning Spell that stuns an opponent, and "stupefy" means "bewilder" or "stun."

10. In *Harry Potter*, "flagrate" causes a wand to leave fiery marks, and the word "conflagration" means "a fire."

11. "Sagacious" means "wise," like a sage.

12. If your intelligence is 16 or better, you might know that Haste is a potion that will get you moving extra fast and buy you an extra action per turn. And "haste" is a great ACT word meaning "speed" or "urgency of movement."

13. When you need to get out fast, Expeditious Retreat is a cheap potion and an easy first-level wizard spell. "Expeditious" means "speedy."

Skill 27 (page 73)

Say What?

1. **D** Refer to your circled key words or scan the passage to locate these answers in the passage. The second paragraph is about Levi-Strauss and mentions one of his publications and compares him to Derrida. The third paragraph tells that Derrida criticized Levi-Strauss. Choice D is correct—we have not been told what languages Derrida has learned.

2. **H** The first paragraph states that Derrida sought "not to reveal . . . something true . . . but to . . . ruminate on . . ." So he did not seek

absolute truth or clear understanding, but an **exploration**.

3. **A** The lines state that Levi-Strauss tried to work past the contradictions, whereas Derrida works with them, celebrating rather than trying to resolve their tension. In other words, Levi-Strauss wanted a solution, whereas Derrida was comfortable with the contradictions. So choice A is the best paraphrase.

4. **H** This question is similar to question 3. "Celebrating rather than trying to resolve" is a paraphrase for "accepting versus trying to change."

Skill 28 (page 75)

How to Read

If reading the passage took over 3 minutes, review Skill 18 and reread the passage. Anyone can learn to read quickly; remember, you are not reading to memorize details, just to get the gist. When it takes you under 3 minutes, you're ready.

If you absolutely cannot do it in under 3 minutes, no problem, here's your strategy: read for 3 minutes and stop. That'll be enough for you to get some main idea and tone info, without spending too much time. But you have to practice watching the clock and knowing when it's been 3 minutes.

Skill 29 (page 78)

How to Be a Reading Ninja

1. **B** This is a "direct info" question (Skill 20). The final paragraph states that Kabir's "poems eventually became scripture for a number of religious traditions: the Bakhti mystic tradition, the Sufi Islamic tradition and the Sikh tradition." The passage does not state that they were used around the world.

2. **F** This is a "most nearly means" question (Skill 19). The next sentence explains the term. It states that the "philosophic atmosphere was shaped both by **beliefs** of the. . . ." So "philosophical climate" means the "beliefs" or

"intellectual environment." Also, remember from Skill 25 that "philosophy" means "the study of knowledge." The passage does not mention stormy arguments or university gatherings, and while religions are mentioned, there are no religious plans.

3. **B** This is a "Say what?" question (Skill 27). The third paragraph states that Kabir "assigned himself the status of a **disciple**, a man who lived simply in the material world to **meditate upon the human spirit and its relation to the divine**." He sought to understand. There is no mention of isolation, overthrowing a king, or being difficult to understand.

4. **J** This is an "attitude" question (Skill 22). Kabir may have been mysterious and his poetry provocative (stimulating) and stirring, but the mood of the passage is **instructive**. It teaches us about Kabir.

5. **D** This is a "main idea" question (Skill 23). Scan the passage and your circled key words for "mysticism." The author did state that mysticism is philosophical and inspiring, but these are single details. The main idea throughout the passage is that mysticism was widely accepted. The first paragraph tells that mysticism is "**accepted religious practice amongst and across faiths**." And the last sentence of the final paragraph states "the ability of others in the mystic tradition to **cut across ethnic, religious, philosophic and the mundane socio-economic and lingual barriers** . . . ."

Science Skills

Skill 30 (page 83)

How to Read Science

The passage explores TME (total mechanical energy). The two experiments differ because one involves a frictionless track and the other is non-frictionless. You'll see in Posttest II,

when we ask questions based on this passage, that almost every question asks you not about the general theme, but just to read the tables anyway.

Skill 31 (page 85)

How to Read Tables and Graphs

1. **C** Don't get intimidated. If a question sounds complicated, just reread it and do whatever seems obvious. That's the key to ACT Science questions. So the question asks how the temperatures of oxygen and carbon dioxide compare. The dashed line, which represents carbon dioxide, is always **higher** than the solid line, which represents oxygen. So the temperatures for carbon dioxide are always **higher** than the temps for oxygen.

2. **F** The chart shows that at 9 s it reached 29.7%. So it reached 20% before 9 seconds. Notice that you don't even need to know what the table is all about to get the question right!

3. **C** The graph shows that at 0.6 cm, weight is between 4 and 5 lb. Notice that only one answer is in this range. That's how they roll. They don't try to confuse you; they just want to see if you can avoid intimidation and read the graph.

4. **J** Circle the key words in the question if you feel confused. We want to retain heat, so look at the heat retention row on the table. Fiberglass is the only one above 90%. Your eye might see the 0.91 for rayon in the linear expansion row first, but make sure to answer the question, which specifically asks for heat retention.

Skill 32 (page 87)

Up and Down

1. **C** Use the process of elimination. As time increases, the dashed line for carbon dioxide stays the same—it does not go up or down. And the solid line for oxygen goes up.

2. **G** As time goes up, the percent concentration, shown in the second column, goes up. And each new number is approximately double the one before it.

3. **C** On the graph, a 0.2 cm print shows a weight of 3 lb, and a 0.6 cm print shows a weight of 4.5 lb. So that fat rabbit munched his way into gaining 1.5 lb (4.5 − 3 = 1.5) and is ready for the winter. Notice that the math is simple. The ACT Science section will NEVER expect you to do any complex math.

4. **F** Use the process of elimination. The values for heat retention increase from rayon to fiberglass. But the values for linear expansion go down, then up, then down. So there is no noticeable relationship.

Skill 33 (page 89)

Between the Lines

1. **B** Look at the graph and find 0.5 s. It's not labeled, but it's between 0 and 1. Then go up from there until you reach approximately 19.5 degrees. You bump into the solid line, which represents oxygen. The carbon dioxide line is higher up, at approximately 30 degrees. There is no information about nitrogen or helium.

2. **H** This is just like the Tetris example in the Skill 33 section. Now 23% falls between two numbers given on the table. It falls between 15.7 and 30.2. So the time associated with 23% will be between the times associated with the 15.7 and 30.2. Only choice H is between the two.

3. **C** At 0.8 cm, the graph is leveling out, but continuing to rise. If it follows the current pattern, it will go up slightly. Only choice C goes up slightly. Choices A and B are lower, and choice D is too high.

4. **J** A heat retention of 77% would place the material between rayon and wool. But the values for linear expansion do not follow an identifiable pattern, so we cannot predict a value.

Skill 34 (page 91)

The Paragraphs

1. **A** The question just compares two columns in the table, but the "50%" and "1-mile stretch of a two-lane road" make people think that they need to do crazy calculations. However, these terms are just restating the conditions of the experiment! So it really just says, "the amount of mixture needed versus salt alone will be. . . ." And the amount of mixture is always **double** the amount of salt alone.

2. **F** The table does not list "ordinary road salt." When that happens, consult the paragraph. The paragraph tells that "ordinary road salt" is NaCl. So according to the table, as temperature drops, NaCl goes up. That makes sense! When it's cold, you sprinkle more road salt on the sidewalk or driveway.

3. **C** What was the prediction? Refer to the paragraph. The researchers predicted that "a given amount of salt/sand mixture could be used interchangeably with ordinary road salt." But the table shows that the amount of salt/sand needed was not equal, but double.

4. **H** Again, the paragraph tells us that "ordinary road salt" is NaCl in the table. And according to the table, NaCl is applied every 2 hours beginning at −5°C. Notice that the answer is not −9, because −5 is closer to zero than −9 and is where the interval begins.

Skill 35 (page 93)

Don't Be Controlled

1. **D** The paragraph told us that the researchers were testing to see if "a given amount of salt/sand mixture could be used interchangeably with ordinary road salt." Use the process of elimination. Choice A was mentioned in the table but is a part of the results and not the main purpose. Choice B should say "**below** zero," and choice C is irrelevant since the salinity levels were told, in the paragraph, to be equal. Notice that the correct answer is nothing

fancy; it's really the most obvious one. That's how the ACT works. Look for the obvious and don't get intimidated!

2. **F** Don't get intimidated. Remember that they never expect you to use something specific from science class. Just use common sense. Why would you need to apply salt more frequently when it's colder? Use the process of elimination.

(F) the road surface refreezes more quickly—Sure, that makes sense if it's colder.

(G) ~~more salt is needed per application~~—True, but it does not address why we need more applications.

(H) ~~salt is more effective than salt/sand~~—True, but it does not address why we need more applications.

(J) ~~salinity decreases~~—This is the intimidating answer. Many students pick this one because it seems very fancy and hard and sciency. Don't do that. We have no evidence that salinity increases or is even relevant to frequency of application. Pick the answer that makes sense to you. Trust yourself.

3. **D** The salt/sand mixture did not cut down on salt, since they needed twice as much of the mixture per application, keeping the actual pounds of salt the same.

Skill 36 (page 95)

Fight!

1. **C** Scientist 1 states that moose seek out conifer cover for shallow snow and greater availability of shrubs for eating.

2. **H** Both scientists state that moose sought cover because of snow conditions. So in June, when there is no snow, neither scientist would predict that moose would seek conifer cover.

3. **B** At the end of the second paragraph for scientist 2, she or he argued that crust

conditions and not snow depth most affected moose mobility.

4. **F** Both scientists refer to ease of movement. The other choices are either not stated by both scientists or not stated at all. For example, choice G is incorrect because the scientists do not imply that moose always prefer conifers, just that they are useful during winter. And choice J is incorrect because the moose preferred conifer cover in March more than February.

5. **D** Scientist 2's hypothesis is expressed in the second paragraph, "So, it was not the snow depth that attracted the moose to the conifers in March, but the crust conditions." Choice D would best test this crust conditions hypothesis. The other choices are interesting but would not directly test the hypothesis.

Skill 37 (page 99)

How to Be a Science Genius

1. **B** Notice that Table 1 is the table in Experiment 1 and Figure 1 is the graph in Experiment 2. The thermometer placed into the 30°C helium is shown on the graph by the solid line. Go to 25 s and look straight up until you reach the solid line. The solid line passes 25 seconds at around 40°C, so choice B is closest.

2. **H** Don't be intimidated. Lots of students get scared off by this one. But it's just asking you how many degrees the temperature changed per second, that's what °C/s means. Remember our Mantra, if you are stuck, just do whatever seems most obvious. The temperature changed 4 degrees (from 21 to 25°C) during that 1 second. So it changed 4/1 (which is just 4) °C/s.

3. **B** Look at Table 1. Look at the 35°C solution column. Look down the column for the biggest jump between numbers. The biggest jump was from the first to second rows, which represents 1 second to 2 seconds. (Remember that the thermometer started at 15°, so the jump from 0 to 1 s was only 4°.)

4. **J** This is another great example of "do what seems obvious." It would be pretty easy to convince yourself that this is some specific concept that you were supposed to have memorized from chemistry class. But remember, you need nothing memorized. Just use common sense. When would atoms move most slowly? When they are least hot. Hot atoms jump all over and cold ones chill out. That's where the phrase "chill out" comes from! So the coldest atoms would move most slowly. Look at the graph to find the coldest that the temperature in the 30°C helium (solid line) gets. Choice J is correct since the solid line gets lowest at 40 s.

5. **A** Figure 1 shows that the thermometer in the 30°C helium took about 18 s to get to 40°C. And it shows that the thermometer in the 15°C helium took about 10 s. So the thermometer in 5°C helium would cool even faster, less than 20 s.

6. **H** The paragraph tells us that thermometer had an initial temperature of **45°C**. So the thermometer will not be heated or cooled in the **45°C beaker of helium**. This is the one used to test if the temperature remained constant. If the thermometer changed in this beaker, it would show that the helium was cooling over time, which would affect the results of the experiment. This element of the experiment that is unchanged is called the "control."

7. **A** In Table 1, as time passes, all samples increase in temperature. Thus, since kinetic energy increases as temperature increases, as time passes and temperature increases, kinetic energy must also increase.

Essay Skills

Skill 38 (page 103)

Brainstorm

Answers will vary, but we want specifics, not generalizations. We want names, dates, places, numbers, statistics, etc. Coming up with specifics at this stage will definitely improve the essay. The more specific the details, the more powerful the argument and the higher your score.

Here's an example of a specific detail that one of my students, Ian Curtis, used for the second prompt:

> High school students in the United States are often considered behind high school students in European and Asian countries. In France, for example, a typical school day begins at eight and doesn't finish until usually five in the evening.

Rather than a generalization about the school day, he offers a very specific example. We'll see how he used this example in the solutions to come.

Skill 39 (page 105)

Brain Freeze Help

Answers vary.

Here are examples with specific details for each prompt:

1. Some school administrators believe that there is no harm in advertisements on campus since students are already exposed to the advertisements outside of school.

   > Students are surrounded with advertisements outside of school. In fact, for most students it's difficult to distinguish between truth and advertisement. If you're hungry "Snickers really satisfies." And, for refreshment, join "the Coke side of life." That is the very reason that school must be a safe zone.

   Others believe that schools should ban advertisements on campus because students learn best in a neutral, ad-free environment, without corporations trying to sway their opinions.

   > For learning to happen, students must be able to open up to and trust what they receive in school. When they learn in health class that they should eat four servings of vegetables per day, they must be able to believe it. For them to take that in, they must be able to trust the messages they hear, even in the cafeteria. If they see any messages at school as marketing slogans engineered to win their purchase, faith in learning is undermined.

2. These schools believe that students will be safer when supervised on campus than when allowed to leave at 2 p.m.

> Most students I know do not leave school and hit the streets. First of all, most kids stay on campus anyway for sports practices or club meetings. But, of the kids who do leave, every one of them that I know either heads home to a parent or to a part-time job. I know four kids that work at the local CVS and five that work at fast-food restaurants. I think these kids would get in more trouble in a after-school study hall or unstructured after-school recess than at their supervised jobs.

Other schools believe that the school day is already too long and that students can handle the responsibility of managing their time until working parents get home.

> The kids who work would be denied the ability to make the extra money that matters very much to them, and in some cases, their families. If there are kids that do not stay for sports and clubs, do not go home to a parent, and do not work, they are probably just spending time with friends (likely supervised by someone else's parent) or doing homework. The very rare kid who's getting into trouble would find a way (possibly even more easily) if s/he was forced to stay at school.

Skill 40 (page 107)

Outline

Answers vary. Circle or jot down the best details. Each will be the focus of a body paragraph.

Skill 41 (page 109)

Write Your Intro

Answers vary. Use opener, link, and thesis. And within that framework let your own particular brilliance, interests, and style shine.

Here's the intro that Ian wrote for the second prompt:

> I would like to preface this essay by saying that I am a teenager, and that anybody responding to this question is a teenager, by definition, since they are taking the ACT. We therefore have a certain interest in

this topic, and are in no way objective. In answering the question of whether or not the school day should be extended, I believe that nearly any student would say no, thank you, I have enough school, thanks. That being said, I think that there are several ways to approach this issue.

Notice that it's not perfect. But graders don't expect a perfect essay in 40 minutes. He opens with an interesting lead-in: How can he be objective—who wants more school? Then he takes his stance. And, finally, he acknowledges that there is, however, complexity to the issue. That's great! Readers are trained to give points for complexity. We'll discuss this more in Skill 45. Acknowledging complexity does not mean taking a weak stance. Keep a strong stance, but give a nod to the depth of the issue.

Skill 42 (page 111)

Transition Sentences

Answers vary. Does your transition sentence accomplish one or more of the following? Introduce the main idea of the paragraph, link to the previous paragraph, and remind us of your thesis.

Here's Ian's transition sentence for his first body paragraph:

> Firstly, the argument could be made, and I would agree with it, that students, especially in high school, need to learn how to live independently and not under supervision.

Great link from the intro to the body, and he sets up the topic of the paragraph—independence.

Skill 43 (page 113)

A Strong Body

Answers vary. Is your body paragraph written around a single main idea? Is it jam-packed with specific details?

Here is Ian's first body paragraph:

> Firstly, the argument could be made, and I would agree with it, that students, especially in high school, need to learn how to live independently and not under supervision. In so many cases there is no room for transition between kids living at home, always under

their parents' watchful eyes, with curfews and rules and the rest, and college. At some point parents need to trust their children because sooner or later, they will most likely end up living in a dorm, completely out of their parents' control, and it is the kids that have never had a taste of freedom that do foolish things once they are finally free of their parents tyrannical reigns.

He sets up a specific situation. Kids need to experience some independence before college so that they know how to handle it in college. This is a strong paragraph. It begins with a transition that establishes the main idea. The vocab and sentence structure are strong (Skill 47). And he reaches a conclusion, demonstrating a point that clearly supports his thesis. He's pretty specific and could take it even further by providing a specific example of this situation in the following paragraph.

Skill 44 (page 115)

More Body

Answers vary. Does your next body paragraph(s) continue demonstrating your thesis? Is it focused on a specific example? Does it begin with a transition sentence that smoothly links it to the previous body paragraph?

Here are Ian's next two body paragraphs:

Secondly, I can see a brilliant solution that might benefit everyone. Start schools later. Although I don't remember the sources, I have read in more than one place that studies have been conducted to test students' productivity at different hours of the day. These tests show that students are significantly better able to perform academically later in the day. I believe that students would get a great deal more out of a school day that ran from eleven to five, as opposed to one that began at eight and finished at two.

Parents that feel that their children should be occupied between the end of classes and their return from work should consider encouraging their kids to get involved in sports, student government, or any of the countless opportunities available in high schools that are not only amusing and rewarding, but also make students very attractive to colleges.

Great paragraphs. Fine transition. Great specifics and nice focus. Ian actually quotes a study! Quote a study, and your score goes up, guaranteed. He also offers a new solution to the problem. Brilliant, more points! Graders love a new solution. These are nice paragraphs organized around main ideas.

Skill 45 (page 117)

Body III

Answers vary. If you add a body paragraph that paraphrases and then disproves the opposite stance on the issue you gain a point.

Ian used two paragraphs for this:

I will concede there could possibly be advantages in a longer school day. High school students in the United States are often considered behind high school students in European and Asian countries. In France, for example, a typical school day begins at eight and doesn't finish until usually five in the evening.

This method, however, would not work so well in the United States. Unlike in France, our classes in high school are largely focused on class discussion and public speaking, activities that may not take as long as test-taking. The fact that our European peers may outperform us on test-taking doesn't surprise me, since their education systems put a much more heavy focus on test-taking. In the end, I would argue that test-taking does not necessarily constitute academic competency, and frankly isn't realistic for real-life application. When will we be asked later in life to, in under an hour, summarize the bill of rights? I suggest it might be more useful to be able to think and talk about such topics rather than be able to rattle off the facts that surround them in a short period of time.

Wow! Go Ian. After the first of the two paragraphs, you might have thought, "Oh, no. He's weakening his stance." But then he hits it home! The second of the two paragraphs slams the opposition. At this point, as long as he comes through with anything but an offensive concluding paragraph, you know he has a definite 12! Also, great vocab and specifics.

Skill 46 (page 119)

Conclusion

Answers vary. Does your conclusion restate thesis, link, and end with a bang? I'm not telling you to be boring or predictable; use the framework to build your own masterpiece. But even if there's no time for a masterpiece, just write a few sentences summing up your essay.

Here's Ian's conclusion:

> In conclusion, I don't think that high school students in the U.S. need to spend any more time in school. What's more, it isn't a school's responsibility to baby-sit high school students before their parents get home from work. If parents can't figure out a solution, that's something they should probably work on with their kids.

Ian was running out of time, so he threw down a few sentences. But the sentences accomplish the task. (Most importantly, there must be a conclusion of some kind to get full credit.) His conclusion wraps up the essay and brings us full circle back to his thesis (that the school day should not be extended). He ends with a philosophical take on the issue. Graders loved that. He's saying that the state and schools should not solve family issues. You can agree or disagree, but he gets you thinking.

Skill 47 (page 121)

Other Stuff That Matters

1. a. "Immutable" means "unchanging" or "indisputable."
       Example: Death and taxes are immutable truths.

    b. "Eradicated" means "erased completely."
       Example: Vaccines have nearly eradicated polio.

    c. "Auspicious" means "fortunate" or "lucky."
       Example: The French interest in a Northern victory proved auspicious for Lincoln.

    d. "Superfluous" means "unneeded" or "inessential."
       Example: Critics state that the government overspends on superfluous items.

    e. "Affinity" means "liking" or "inclination."
       Example: Gatsby was known for his large parties, yet he had an affinity for privacy.

    f. "Concordant" means "in agreement."
       Example: The ideas expressed in Lincoln's speech were concordant with his earlier declarations.

    g. "Pertinent" means "relevant."
       Example: Gandhi's way of life is pertinent if we want to understand his politics.

    h. "Thwart" means "to prevent."
       Example: The storm thwarted the thief's plan.

    i. "Ramification" means "effect."
       Example: There were many economic and social ramifications of the Civil War.

2. Answers vary. In your paragraph, did you get deep, write a fair bit, use some impressive vocab, vary your sentences, write readably, and avoid basic grammar and spelling errors?

Skill 48 (page 123)

Proofread

Answers vary. Proofread for omitted words, misspellings, and punctuation errors, and to make sure that you indented, started new paragraphs when you meant to, and wrote details correctly.

Skill 49 (page 125)

How to Be a Writing Monster

Did you use the Skills?

Check your essay, item by item, with this checklist.

If you don't feel confident checking your own essay, ask a parent or teacher to use the list. Check off items that you mastered, and circle items that need improvement.

1. Brainstorm for specific details, not generalizations.

2. If something else brilliant occurs to you, of course use that; but if not, just turn the general viewpoints from the question into specific examples.

3. Jot down or circle the best details from your brainstorm. These details form the outline for the body paragraphs of the essay.

4. Your intro paragraph should be two to four sentences: an opener, a link, and a thesis.

5. Use transition sentences to begin each paragraph, link it to the previous paragraph, and remind the reader of your thesis.

6. Each "body" paragraph begins with a link to the previous paragraph and is written around a single main idea.

7. The last body paragraph paraphrases the opposite view and then disproves it.

8. Structure your conclusion by restating your thesis, linking, and ending with a bang.

9. Get deep, write at least two pages, use some impressive vocab, vary your sentences, write readably, and avoid basic grammar and spelling errors.

10. Leave a few minutes to proofread your essay for omitted words, misspellings, and punctuation errors, and to make sure that you indented, started new paragraphs when you meant to, and wrote details accurately.

Generally, an organized essay will earn at least an 8.

Length, details, depth of analysis (including disproving the opposite view), and cool vocab will earn you a 9 to 12. The more details, depth of analysis, and cool vocab, the higher your score will be.

Skill 50 (page 131)

Brian's Friday Night Spiel

Practice this relaxation technique every day.

Posttest I (page 137)

1. **C** When a verb is underlined, trust your ear. "I have been walking" sounds weird after "one day last year." That's because "last year" is done and tells us that "have been waking" should be "woke."

2. **J** When a verb is underlined, identify the subject and cross out any prepositional phrases; a prepositional phrase NEVER counts as the subject of the verb. "With no results" is a prepositional phrase. So "she" is the subject of the underlined verb, and "she **were** trying" should be "she **was** trying."

3. **B** When a pronoun is underlined, we must be totally sure what noun it is referring to. If it is unclear in any way, it is incorrect. The underlined pronoun must also match (singular or plural) the noun that it refers to. We can't tell if the underlined "she" refers to Jenna or Sapphire. Use the process of elimination. The only answer that corrects the problem is choice B.

4. **G** If a transition word (such as "although," "since," "but," "therefore," or "however") is underlined, see if it works in the flow of the paragraph. "Therefore" implies cause and effect and does not fit into the flow. The sentences are not cause and effect, but in chronological order, so the answer is choice G, "Then." You can also use the process of elimination and see which choice sounds best in the flow of the sentences. Your ear will know!

5. **C** We never need a comma right between a subject "I" and a verb "sat." The comma after "sat" works because "anxiously watching Jenna" is a side note. You can hear the pause when you read it. Also, without the comma it would seem that "anxiously" describes how they sat.

6. **F** "About the shots to come" could not stand alone, so we separate the clauses with commas, not a semicolon. Also, in this case, "however" is a side note and is separated with commas.

7. **B** When a preposition is underlined, ask yourself if it is the right preposition to use. "Woken up **about** a bat" sounds weird. Literally, she "woke up **with** a bat in her room." She did not literally "wake up **from** a bat in her room." That's too slangy.

8. **F** "It's" means "it is," and "its" is possessive, like "that tree is nice; I like its colorful leaves." So "It's" is correct in this sentence. "It's" does not sound terrific in this sentence, but using the process of elimination, it's the best choice.

9. **D** The nurses are not possessing anything, so we do not need the apostrophe s ('s). If one nurse had possessed, we'd use "nurse's," and if more than one had possessed, we'd use "nurses'."

10. **J** The ACT likes crisp and clear; we always want the answer that is most clear, concise, direct, and nonredundant. "Have to be getting" is very wordy. Choice J is most clear and direct.

11. **A** A descriptive phrase on the ACT must be clearly associated with (and usually placed right next to) the noun described. Choice A is correct because the phrase "having trouble finding my vein" is correctly associated with (and next to) "the nurse"—whom it describes. It was not "I" (choice B) or "were" (choice C) that was "having trouble finding my vein," and choice D is wordy and passive.

12. **H** Make sure that the underlined word fits in the context of the sentence. She was not waiting "greatly," "deeply," or "intensely" (powerfully). She was waiting "anxiously."

13. **C** For "flow" questions, use the process of elimination. The underlined portion is hilarious! If it were cut, the passage would lose "a comical anecdote" (a funny story). The underlined portion is not a tie-in to the introduction or a transition.

14. **F** For "goal" questions, choose the one answer choice that achieves the very specific GOAL stated in the question. The very specific goal for this question is to "best introduce the tone and focus of the paragraph." The focus of the paragraph is her nickname, "rabies girl." So choice F is best. All of the other choices are relevant to the passage, but **only** choice F is relevant to that paragraph.

15. **B** A conclusion wraps up an essay. The final paragraph of this passage is a successful conclusion. It wraps up her rabies experience and even offers a lesson that she learned.

16. **H** Use your ear to test the underlined verb. "Today I was felt" sounds strange. Use the process of elimination. Only choice H sounds better, and the underlined verb "was felt" should be "feel." Choice J almost works but is too slangy; it should be "**have** been feeling."

17. **B** The main theme is the importance of communal ownership in art, also called the commons. This is expressed in the title, "The New British Art Culture: Come Together Right Now," as well as in the first and last sentences of many of the paragraphs. The passage is not about controversy between artists and politicians or about art sales. And while choice D, "absurd examples of property rights," is mentioned, it is certainly not the main theme. So you can get this question through the process of elimination. Just make sure to eliminate only answers that are definitely wrong.

18. **H** Scan the passage and your circled key words for "David Bollier." Find evidence. In the sixth paragraph he is described as "one of America's foremost proponents of the commons." He is a proponent, so clearly he approves of and respects it. Don't be fooled by choice G. He does not think there needs to be reform of the commons, but of property rights.

19. **B** Cross out the italicized word and decide what word would make sense in its place. "It does ~~dampen~~ the ability of the artist to speak freely . . ." "It" refers to the system that makes artists into business people, which was earlier said to *reduce* or *diminish* their creative freedom.

20. **F** Scan the passage for the phrase. It's the main idea of the fourth paragraph, so you might have even circled it. Use the process of elimination. The paragraph states that the commons is public ownership, so it is not choice G, tightening private ownership laws, or choice J, increasing government control. Also,

while choice H has words used in the paragraph, it is definitely not the meaning of the phrase. Make sure to choose an answer supported by evidence in the passage, and not just because several words match.

21. **D** The first paragraph suggests that McRobbie disagrees with the government's actions by stating that the new system is pushing artists into "insecurity." This is further supported in the second paragraph where McRobbie believes that the new system limits artists' freedom.

22. **H** In the final paragraph, the author states that the promoters are NOT trying to separate the artists from property, meaning they are not trying to steal. He states that they are trying to prevent people's attempts of controlling what should belong to everyone. If that seemed confusing, just keep reading the passage. He goes on to state, "the commons can help set arts in a new and **free** direction." Remember that difficult lines in a passage are always explained nearby!

23. **A** The main purpose is to explore the concept of the commons and its appeal. This is supported by the title and the first and last lines of most paragraphs. You can also scan the key words that you circled to get a sense of the main idea. Don't be confused by answers that contain words from the passage but are not the main idea. For example, the words "market-driven" appear in the second paragraph; you may have even circled them. But they describe what the author is against and are not the main idea.

24. **J** McRobbie's essay introduces the "topic of concern" that mainstreaming art limits artistic freedom. In the rest of the passage, this issue is not consistently paraphrased (restated), debunked (discredited), or refuted. It is explored and taken further.

25. **B** Find evidence. All of the answers seem reasonable, but the passage specifically states "as a result . . . a higher social currency . . . can

stifle (limit) **their own original voices**." So it might give them more status and opportunity, but not more artistic freedom.

26. **J** Cross out the italicized word and decide what word would make sense in its place: "while we acknowledge Dylan's unique and ~~vital~~ voice, we also see that he built of other sources." Also, always read before and after the line referenced. The sentences before stated that "Bob Dylan is a genius who shaped American music." So the point of the lines is that Dylan had a "voice" that was *very important* in shaping American music. You can also use the process of elimination. You may think that Dylan was lively, vigorous, or brisk, but there is no evidence in the passage for those words.

27. **C** Scan the passage and your circled key words for a definition of the commons or where it was introduced. The fourth paragraph describes it: "The commons exist outside of either private or government control. They are public. . . . " Use the process of elimination. It is not owned by the government or corporations, so it must be choice C, a free collaboration.

28. **F** The first two paragraphs state that McRobbie disagrees with the government's actions and that the new system is pushing artists into "insecurity" and limiting artists' freedom: "it does dampen the ability of the artist to speak freely. . . ."

29. **B** Scan the passage and your circled key words for "Bob Dylan." Find evidence. The fifth paragraph states that "Bob Dylan is a genius who shaped American music, but his work was inspired by the American folk music tradition and biblical literature and poetry. Dylan's music does not stand separate from any of these currents. . . . he built of other sources." So he is not an imposter or truly original, but drew from sources to create something new. Also, there is no evidence at all for choice D, regarding Dylan and property laws.

30. **J** The numbers of abdominal markings for the four wasps, in order of number of markings, are A: 2, D: 2, B: 3, and C: 4. But the ordering of wasps according to wingspan or age is not in the same order, so there is no correlation.

31. **A** Look at Experiment 2. Table 2 tells us that wasp B was never dominant. If you scan the table, you never see "B dominant." It backed away from all its interactions.

32. **J** Compare the order of wasps according to age (B, C, D, A from youngest to oldest) to the order of wasps according to number of abdominal spots (A/D, B, C from least to most). The orderings are completely different, so there is no pattern, and age does not relate to or have an effect on number of markings.

33. **A** The order of wingspans from least to greatest is B, D, A, C. This matches the order of dominance, or the order of number of dominant interactions for the wasps. So the larger the wingspan, the more dominant. And since 13 mm would make the fifth wasp the largest, the data imply that that wasp would be most dominant.

34. **G** The A column in Experiment 2 shows that wasp A was dominant two times, against wasp B and wasp D, and that it backed away one time, against wasp C.

35. **D** As stated in the solution to question #30, the order of wasps according to number of abdominal markings does not match the order according to dominance, so number of markings and dominance do not consistently correlate.

36. **G** Experiment 1 records wingspan, age, and number of markings, whereas Experiment 2 records the dominance results of interactions.

37. **A** Just choose a point on the graph and see which characteristic it matches. For example, at age 2 on the graph, the y axis (the vertical axis) shows approximately 12. According to the table, an age of 2 has a wingspan of 12 and 4 abdominal markings. So the vertical axis must be wingspan, not abdominal markings. Nondominance and weight are never mentioned.

38.–49. Did you use the Skills?
Check your essay, item by item, with this checklist. If you don't feel confident checking your own essay, ask a parent or teacher to use the list. Check off items that you mastered, and circle items that need improvement.

1. Brainstorm for specific details, not generalizations.

2. If something else brilliant occurs to you, of course use that; but if not, just turn the general viewpoints from the question into specific examples.

3. Jot down or circle the best details from your brainstorm. These details form the outline for the body paragraphs of the essay.

4. Your intro paragraph should be 2 to 4 sentences: an opener, a link, and a thesis.

5. Use transition sentences to begin each paragraph, link it to the previous paragraph, and remind the reader of your thesis.

6. Each "body" paragraph begins with a link to the previous paragraph and is written around a single main idea.

7. The last body paragraph paraphrases the opposite view and then disproves it.

8. Structure your conclusion by restating your thesis, linking, and ending with a bang.

9. Get deep, write at least two pages, use some impressive vocab, vary your sentences, write readably, and avoid basic grammar and spelling errors.

10. Leave a few minutes to proofread your essay for omitted words, misspellings, and punctuation errors, and to make sure that you indented, started new paragraphs when you meant to, and wrote details accurately.

Generally, an organized essay will earn at least an 8.

Length, details, depth of analysis (including disproving the opposite view), and cool vocab will earn you a 9 to 12. The more details, depth of analysis, and cool vocab, the higher your score will be.